Nazi Cinema

Erwin Leiser

CinemaTwo

[NAZI CINEMA]

Erwin Leiser
Translated from the German by
Gertrud Mander and David Wilson

Secker & Warburg
London

Nazi Cinema by Erwin Leiser
first published in 1968 by Rowohlt Taschenbuch Verlag GmbH, Hamburg
This English-language edition translated by Gertrud Mander and David Wilson
first published in Great Britain in 1974 by
Martin Secker and Warburg Limited
14 Carlisle Street, London W1V 6NN
Copyright © Secker and Warburg 1974

SBN 436 09708 7 (hardcover)
      436 09709 5 (paperback)

Filmset in Photon Times 11 on 12pt by
Richard Clay (The Chaucer Press), Ltd, Bungay, Suffolk
and printed in Great Britain by
Fletcher & Son, Ltd, Norwich

Contents

Kolberg

Introduction

This book was written while I was working on a compilation film on the same theme: propaganda in the film of the Third Reich. My film was confined to showing the use of feature films in the openly political propaganda programme of the Third Reich. The totalitarian system's abuse of the mass media demonstrates just how necessary is the democratic social structure and the right to freedom of information which that system opposes.

The film *Deutschland, erwache!* (*Wake up, Germany!*) is made up of sequences selected from feature films and presented as documentary evidence. There is very little commentary, and only very occasionally are the distortions which these films make juxtaposed with the truth. These sequences, which I have classified as propaganda and arranged in some kind of order, are in themselves enough to expose the workings of National Socialist propaganda. To have presented them more explicitly would only have prompted some kind of emotional reaction, and might thereby have activated in many viewers a defence mechanism and a readiness to suppress the truth. Because things are left unsaid in the film, the viewer is placed in an emotional vacuum and obliged to adopt a personal, critical attitude towards the material. It is thus impossible for an audience to identify unthinkingly either with the propaganda contained in the film sequences or with my own comments. No value judgments are made; this is left to the viewer. There is no mention of names, since it is the subject which is important. The material must be judged in a contemporary light.

This book substantially supplements the film, in that it is not confined to feature films and overt propaganda but is also an attempt to analyse the major characteristics of Nazi film as a whole. Themes which are characteristic – and characteristic not only of this period – are illustrated by individual examples. But it is not my intention to describe the whole history of film in the Third Reich.

I have seen all the films mentioned in the book, though it was often difficult to find prints, which are dispersed throughout the world and often preserved in an incomplete form. For both the film and the book I managed to find, in various archives, hundreds of feature films and documentaries and thousands of newsreels made during the Third Reich. Appropriate material from other countries was referred to for comparison, and every Nazi film was examined with regard to the actual political situation at the time it was made and shown. I was also able to examine scripts as well as documents on the production of particular films and public reaction to them.

Everyone who works on this period knows the difficulty of interpreting source material correctly. It goes without saying, for example, that the diaries kept by the Propaganda Minister are indispensable for a complete under-standing of his political attitudes. But they were not destined simply for the author's private use; they were intended to be read by his own and later generations, with the aim of establishing an official, refurbished portrait of Goebbels. Clearly the contents of the diaries must be closely examined, but confirmation is very often impossible. Comparison of statements made after the war by high-ranking officials with documents from the Third Reich reveals a clear contradiction between their attitudes before 1945 and what they said later. More often than one might credit, people played a double bluff, trying to win the trust of both the Third Reich authorities *and* their enemies. Many of them must have been struck by the disagreeable realisation that their films might survive the brownshirt regime, and even before the collapse of Hitler's Reich they were preparing to justify themselves. In many cases substantiating a fact or checking a statement can only be arrived at accidentally, for example by comparing a later statement with an earlier document which the person in question does not know about or thinks has disappeared. But it was not my concern to unearth scandal about the leaders of the time nor to pry into their private lives; when I mention an individual it is only by way of example. My purpose is to demonstrate, as clearly as I can, the mechanics by which film became part of the propaganda machine.

I have chosen sequences from both notorious and forgotten films, films which are still banned because their propaganda is still effective and films which have been classified as harmless, in order to illustrate the use made of film by a totalitarian system. A number of the arguments employed by Nazi propaganda against the parliamentary system are being revived in the present-day political scene. The Third Reich is not the only regime to organise crude propaganda by dressing up lies as statements of fact. An audience of today may laugh at passages which Third Reich audiences fell for under the spell of propaganda; and may repeatedly ask itself how it was possible for people not to see through the lies. But only too often the laughter sticks in the throat.

The title of the film and the original German edition of the book takes a slogan from the early years of National Socialism – 'Wake up, Germany!' – and turns it against Hitler and his spiritual heirs. Shortly before the Nazis seized power, *Simplicissimus** published a cartoon showing Germany as a little old woman shouting from her window to a rowdy mob of stormtroopers in the street below: 'How can I sleep when you're making all that noise?' Hitler's speeches and His Master's obedient Voice, the Goebbels propaganda machine, painted the devil black to create an image of the 'Führer' as an archangel and his henchmen as crusaders. In the meeting halls and on the streets of the Weimar Republic the brownshirt battalions raised their battle-cries, and the unpolitical German public were terrified. Drunk with sleep, they were easily steered in the required direction, with the truth concealed and any undesirable thought process obstructed. It was necessary to produce a state of panic, permanent fear of an enemy who went under many names and who was made responsible for every adversity and every failure.

Behind a slogan like 'Wake up, Germany!' was concealed its opposite. The object was to put to sleep conscience, independent thought, belief in freedom and human dignity. Responsibility for the state rested with a 'Führer' who was accountable to no one, and at whose discretion an individual could be reduced to an object. Moral values were annulled in the name of a new morality, as the words of the cry 'Wake up, Germany!' were drunkenly travestied.

The Nazis soon removed the comma from this slogan: the words 'Wake up Germany' were to be an indissoluble unit. Here I have reinstated the comma. In doing so, I have given the title of my film and this book the sense of a challenge, whose justification is the material I have assembled here.

E. L.

* A satirical newspaper.

1. The Joseph Goebbels Programme

On 11 March 1933, the Hitler government decided to establish a Ministry for 'popular enlightenment and propaganda'. The head of this momentously designated new Ministry was to be responsible for film, as well as for all other cultural activities in the Third Reich. On 28 March 1933, Goebbels addressed the representatives of the German film industry for the first time. He outlined his models; and though he did not venture to quote directly from Lenin, who had said that 'of all the arts film is for us the most important', he did have this to say about Eisenstein's *Battleship Potemkin*: 'It is a marvellously well made film, and one which reveals incomparable cinematic artistry. Its uniquely distinctive quality is the line it takes. This is a film which could turn anyone with no firm ideological convictions into a Bolshevik. Which means that a work of art can very well accommodate a political alignment, and that even the most obnoxious attitude can be communicated if it is expressed through the medium of an outstanding work of art.'

In the same speech Goebbels named three other films which had made 'an indelible impression' on him. He singled out Garbo's performance in *Anna Karenina* as a demonstration of 'an intrinsically cinematic art'. He described Luis Trenker's *The Rebel* as a film which could 'overwhelm even a non-National Socialist'. And of Fritz Lang's *The Nibelungen* he said: 'Here is an

Hitler and Goebbels at a film première

epic film not of our time, and yet so modern, so contemporary, so topical, that even the stalwarts of the National Socialist movement were deeply moved.' He omitted to mention that he had just banned Fritz Lang's latest film, *The Testament of Dr Mabuse*, in which the terror tactics and slogans of the brownshirt brigades had been unmasked. He warned that the new movement would not be wasting its energy on parades and fanfares: 'There are many people who will have to realise that when the flag goes down the bearer goes down with it.' He described the Nazi seizure of power as a turning-point in film production; from now on 'the only possible art is one which is rooted in the soil of National Socialism'.

Hitler himself had clearly defined the objectives of National Socialist propaganda in *Mein Kampf*. 'The first responsibility of a new movement based on a foundation of popular ideology is therefore to ensure that an understanding of the essence and function of the State is given clear and uniform expression.' In his book *Childhood and Society*,* Erik H. Erikson

* W. W. Norton, New York, 1963.

11

has convincingly shown how 'the combination of personal revelation and shrewd propaganda (together with loud and determined action) at last carried with it that universal conviction for which the smouldering rebellion in German youth had been waiting: that no old man, be he father, emperor, or god, need stand in the way of his love for his mother Germany. At the same time it proved to the grown-up men that by betraying their rebellious adolescence they had become unworthy of leading Germany's youth, which henceforth would "shape its own destiny". Both fathers and sons now could identify with the Führer, an adolescent who never gave in.'

A Hitler Youth film called *March to the Führer* shows Hitler Youth members leaving their grey everyday lives to carry their flags to the Nuremberg Rally, the Führer's big parade. A celebrated director, who made his name during the Third Reich, described to me how he had asked a Hitler Youth leader what the Third Reich meant and was told 'Marching together'. The old moral principles were replaced by simple formulae. Thus the official definition in the law establishing the Chamber of Culture: 'Hitherto the state *controlled* the individual; the new state will *incorporate him.*'

Hitler wanted to exploit film entirely for propaganda purposes, but 'in such a way that every filmgoer will know: today I am going to see a political film'. Goebbels preferred a different method. Of the approximately 1,150 feature films produced during the Third Reich, only about one-sixth were straight political propaganda. But every film had a political function. The entertainment films made during the Third Reich did not feature even the Nazi salute, because it was simpler to let a non-political audience go on believing that the old, cosy idyll still prevailed. There was much talk of realism, but a realistic portrayal of everyday life was avoided. That might have been dangerous: people were to be manipulated without being shown the direction in which they were being led. Which explains why Goebbels was not particularly interested in explicit glorification of the Nazi movement in films. No one must be allowed to get the impression that the revolution was over.

Alfred Rosenberg, the Party theoretician, who repeatedly and unsuccessfully sought to dispute Goebbels' authority, was not the only Party veteran to reject the Propaganda Minister's indirect tactics. In his political diary, on 11 December 1939, Rosenberg noted how forcefully Hitler had criticised Goebbels' film policy. Once, at table, Goebbels referred to Karl Ritter's films as 'good national cinema'; Hitler answered, irritably according to Rosenberg: 'Yes, some of them are patriotic in a general sense, but none of them are National Socialist.' Another entry in Rosenberg's diary, dated 8 March 1940, noted the lack 'in these times of a firm, steadfast conviction ... Dr Goebbels, who so often talks of spiritual warfare, may find the right tone for a

' Kitsch: *Befreite Hände*

company of Levantines, but not for the German people. With the war on our very doorstep, the so-called film industry was turning out indiscriminately pro-British films like *Lied der Wüste* [*Desert Song*]; now we have the highly tendentious pro-Irish fashion (*Fuchs von Glenarvon*) [*The Fox of Glenarvon*], and with it the obnoxious kitsch of daughter–father problems (*Weg zu Isabel*) [*The Way to Isabel*]. A mishmash like *Befreite Hände* [*Liberated Hands*] is considered real art, and imitations of pre-war Paris like *Nanette* and *Ihr erstes Erlebnis* [*Her First Experience*] are thought to be fetching and popular . . .'

Hitler had realised at an early stage that in Germany revolutionary change is only possible after the establishment of a legal government. Goebbels knew that in excessive doses overt political propaganda would be ineffectual, and so he let his poison work insidiously. The Goebbels programme was to have life itself providing the content of films; his dream was to portray the Third Reich's problems in a National Socialist version of *Battleship Potemkin*. It was this which prompted the creator of *Battleship Potemkin*, Sergei Eisenstein, to whom Goebbels had more than once referred in flattering terms, to publish an open letter to Goebbels in *Literaturnaja Gazeta* on 22 March 1934. Among other things, Eisenstein demanded:

How dare you of all people talk about life — you who are inflicting death and exile on all things living and good in your country with the axe and the machine-gun; you who are executing the finest sons of the German proletariat, who are forcing the pride of true German science and universal culture to scatter all over the world? How dare you call on your film-makers for a true representation of life without also requiring them, as their very first duty, to cry aloud to the world the sufferings of the thousands of people languishing in the underground catacombs of your jails, tortured to death in your prison barracks?

The 'coordination'* of the German cinema was effected behind the scenes, by a process of which the outsider was largely unaware. Goebbels controlled the department which licensed every film before work on it could begin; which decided whether the completed film could be released for public distribution; and which, in the case of films considered important by the government, selected the actors, provided complete or partial finance, awarded special categories to completed films to attract audiences, and allowed tax concessions. Goebbels' intervention was either direct or through the *Reichsdramaturg*.† A Department of Film, initially established on 14 July 1933 as a temporary authority, was incorporated as a unit of the Chamber of Culture on 22 September 1933. It comprised ten divisions:

I. General Administration
    (i) Legal
    (ii) Budget and Finance
    (iii) Personnel
II. Politics and Culture
    (i) Domestic Press Service
    (ii) Foreign Press Service
    (iii) State Film Archive
III. Artistic Supervision of Film Production
    (i) Script Advisers
    (ii) Casting
IV. Film Industry
    Special department: Foreign exchange business
    Special department: Laws of copyright, labour and tax
V. Film Profession
    Membership in 12 branches:
      Producers
      Directors
      Art Directors
      Production Managers

* *Gleichschaltung*, National Socialist terminology for the obligatory assimilation within the state of all political, economic and cultural activities.

† A state official whose function was to vet scripts.

Cameramen
Sound engineers
Editors
Actors
Extras
Make-up
Properties
Wardrobe
VI. Production Department
    (i) Feature films
    (ii) Export
    (iii) Studios
VII. Domestic Distribution Department
VIII. Cinemas
IX. Technical Department, film and cinemas
X. Department of art films, commercials and film agencies

One of the organs of the State Film Department was the Film Credit Bank. Some State Film Department officials also held positions in the film section of the National Socialist Propaganda Directorate, which was also responsible to Goebbels and which, in 1936, had at its disposal over 32 provincial, 771 district and 22,357 local film agencies.

The film industry was nationalised in stages. A serious crisis in the mid-Thirties, caused by falling export revenue and increased production costs, enabled the Nazi authorities to nationalise the film companies. And in the Spring of 1942, all film companies were placed under one central administration.

Veit Harlan described Goebbels as an omnipresent, demonic dictator of film, justifying his own work as a director during the Third Reich on the ground that as a director he was simply not responsible for the content of his films. But Wolfgang Liebeneiner told me, in a conversation in Frankfurt on 8 April 1965, that it was possible to resist the Minister's patronage and even sabotage unequivocally political projects. He described to me the so-called 'Minister's copy', a treatment of each film prepared especially for Goebbels. There are many examples of how Third Reich directors managed to bypass the Minister's instructions.

Among the films which deviated from the official formula were *Romanze in Moll* (*Romance in a Minor Key*, 1943), *Grosse Freiheit Nr. 7* (*The Great Freedom, No. 7*, 1944)* and *Unter den Brücken* (*Under the Bridges*, 1945),

---

* The word *Freiheit* was avoided during the Third Reich, except in the Nietzschean sense of the state's 'freedom' to act on the individual's behalf. The words 'Nr. 7', referring to an address, were therefore added to the film's title to avoid any misunderstanding.

all directed by Helmut Käutner. These films uphold the individual's right to a life unfettered by the demands of discipline, emphasising an independence in the private domain which invalidates the Führer's authoritarian claims on the individual, which required a complete submission of the self to the community. In addition to these celebrated examples of the kind of 'interior emigration' which even during the war could appear in German films, I should also mention Harald Braun's *Nora* (1944). Here the woman of the film is not the familiar faithful subject of an omniscient husband; she is actually better equipped than he is to cope with the realities of life. In contrast to the original character in Ibsen's play, the rich and powerful Johannes Brack is given some mildly Jewish characteristics (he is played by the actor who plays Nathan Rothschild in the anti-semitic *The Rothschilds*); but unlike other Jewish characters in the films of the period, he is neither comic nor brutal: 'I am not myself evil – it was the evil in society which forced me to be so.' He wants 'only to be a human being among other human beings', and dreams of the love and affection which are denied him.

It was not because of sabotage that the Propaganda Minister's vision of a National Socialist *Battleship Potemkin* or a German *Mrs Miniver* remained unfulfilled. In a world where human relationships were determined by the rank displayed on a uniform, where the Führer was everything and the individual nothing, it was impossible to make a film about everyday life on the lines of the 1942 film about the Miniver family. Films made to glorify an episode in Nazi history required a hero figure, a leader surrounded by the faithful; whereas the Soviet film pays homage to the anonymous revolutionary, and to a mass movement in which the individual can show his face. When he was asked to name the best of German cinema, Goebbels, far from identifying some political epic, mentioned the comedy *Wenn wir alle Engel wären* (*If we were all Angels*), and even Josef von Sternberg's *Blue Angel*, which predates the Nazi seizure of power and which contradicts both the ideology and the racial laws of the Third Reich.

Goebbels' most important political weapon was the newsreel. But the entertainment film was by no means 'considered inferior because it had no message', as the director Arthur Maria Rabenalt emphasises in his book *Film in Zwielicht* (*Film in Twilight*), published fifteen years after the collapse of the Hitler régime and concerned with 'the Third Reich's non-political cinema and the limitations of totalitarian pressure'. Rabenalt refers to 'the dilemma confronting the non-political film of the period', which had to be unrealistic in order to remain 'non-political'. What he does not say is that in the Third Reich it was just not possible to make 'non-political' films. Goebbels knew exactly why he could not make openly political use of entertainment films,

... reitet für Deutschland: anti-semitic caricature in a scene cut after the war

whose function was to distract the audience from reality and lull them to sleep, generally by means of the battery of clichés manufactured in the arsenal of Nazi propaganda.

Rabenalt is pleading his own cause when he maintains that it is 'the involuntary, unintentional effect produced by a film' which makes it political. 'A sports film about a tournament rider, whose sentiments were straightforwardly patriotic and which was made with no political intent, assumed political proportions simply because of its success in neutral and occupied countries as well as at home. The result was that the film [... *reitet für Deutschland (Riding for Germany ...*)] was subsequently awarded the "politically distinguished" category;* was counted, after the collapse of Germany, among the most notorious Nazi films on the blacklist; and earned its director and its leading actors an almost two-year professional ban by the Americans (while Harro, the film's horse, was deported by the Russians). When the tidal wave of emotion had subsided, the film was considered

---

* The German government, then as now (in West Germany), operates a quality aid system whereby certain outstanding films are awarded a *Prädikat*, which reduces or in some cases entirely remits the entertainment tax.

. . . reitet für Deutschland: 'An unconditional faith in him and his mission' (Gerhild Weber, Willy Birgel)

harmless and non-political, and as one of the first to be struck off the Allied list of banned films was successfully released for the third time.'

On 20 September 1952, *Filmecho* reported on the release of Arthur Maria Rabenalt's *Riding for Germany* . . .: 'Now released by the FSK with minor cuts involving some anti-semitic and nationalist scenes.' In 1941, *Filmwelt* (in its 11 July issue) had considered these scenes – not mentioned by Rabenalt – important enough to say in its review of the film: 'There are masterpieces of cameo acting by Willi Rose, Paul Dahlke, Rudolf Schündler and particularly Herbert Hübner as the Jewish bookmaker and Walter Lieck as the horse dealer.' Hübner dominates a scene, cut after the war, which for grotesque anti-semitic caricature has few equals. In its account of the early Twenties the film employs familiar clichés. The former officer and debt-ridden landowner fares badly, of course, in a world where miserable civilians insist on having their loans repaid. As a gentleman rider he is naturally above working with his own hands on his estate. And the film takes his side. He enters a riding tournament in Switzerland and wins not only the first prize but a quantity of solid Swiss francs, with which he reclaims his estate. A newspaper described the scene: 'Like a bronze statue to German power and might, horse and rider stand motionless before this international forum.'

The successful rider is one of the many solitary leader figures in the films of the period – a man who expects from the woman he loves an unconditional faith in him and his mission (riding for Germany). Like Hitler, who said that he went 'the way providence told me to go', with the sure-footedness of a sleepwalker, the gentleman rider knows what he must do, knows that he must 'listen to the voice inside me which commands . . . It is destiny, just as it was destiny which lost us the war even though we were victorious.' Since a leader needs someone to lead, he has a loyal retainer – 'one of my best NCOs'. In one of the scenes cut after the war, this bold individualist is confronted by an uncomprehending representative of the Weimar Republic, characterised by a portrait on the wall of the Social Democrat President Ebert.

The accumulation of clichés and of this kind of notion of moral worth in the so-called 'non-political' films of the Third Reich is the rule rather than the exception. Even films where Third Reich thinking is not so thickly laid on as in *Riding for Germany* . . . make their contribution towards steering the audience in the required direction. Americans smoke fat cigars, drink whisky and never take their hats off, even in the living-room. Certain professional classes – bankers, hoteliers, newspaper publishers – can't be trusted. A woman who jeopardises a marriage or turns a man into a criminal is seldom blonde. The introductory titles of Karl Hartl's *Gold* (1934) explain the motive for making gold artificially by describing it as 'both the happiness and the curse of our world . . . For gold, kinsmen, tribes, nations go to war; for gold, men cheat, persecute, slaughter each other.' In conversation during dinner at his headquarters on 26 February 1942, Hitler pronounced on a film whose lovers' dialogue would be taken by a contemporary audience as expressing an alarming blend of helplessness and cruelty, and thus as a statement of a prevailing prejudice of the time. 'The Rumanian peasant,' he said, 'is nothing but a miserable head of cattle. Everything else on display represents beyond a doubt the most contemptible breed of men. The film *Stadt Anatol* [*The Town of Anatol*] has caught the milieu of this Balkan oil development really well. People who find themselves the owners of a running gold supply without doing a stroke of work, just because there happens to be an oil deposit under their land – that's completely against the natural order.'

The objective of brownshirt propaganda, which included film from the outset, is contained in the warning Goebbels put into an order of the day for the 'Unknown Stormtrooper': 'Let the German people parade in formation, thirty million cretins, and the eternal Empire of Ahasverus will have dawned.'

2. To die for Germany

On 2 February 1933, two days after being appointed Chancellor of the Reich, Hitler attended the première of *Morgenrot* (*Dawn*), a Ufa film about the adventures of a submarine commander and his crew during the First World War. In retrospect there is something symbolic in the fact that the film which Hitler saw at the dawn of the Thousand Year Reich, should have outlined the major theme of Nazi propaganda: to die for Germany.

In the film's central scene the submarine is sinking, and for the ten survivors there are only eight escape suits. The captain suggests that he and his first officer should go down with the ship and the crew should save itself. The crew rejects the suggestion: 'Either everyone or no one!' The captain asks his first officer whether it would be right to accept this sacrifice, to which the reply is, 'What men are these! I could die ten deaths for Germany, a hundred deaths!' Whereupon the captain thanks his crew with these words: 'We Germans may not know much about living, but we are great at dying. Men, shall we stay together on the other side?'

Characteristically, death is glorified as well as belittled. The captain enjoys the idea of 'marching over there' with his men. But there is to be no hero's death. The first officer – who loves the same girl as his superior officer and has discovered on the ship that she does not share his feelings – and another sailor commit suicide, thus saving their comrades' lives. In later war films of the Third Reich similar conflicts between friends are always resolved in the same way: one of them wins the girl, and the other avoids being a failure in life by dying a hero's death. Paul, the sailor in *Dawn*, is another outsider who has never known love and can only give meaning to his life by sacrificing it; he will reappear on the screen in numerous variations. In a film about airmen during the Second World War there is a dare-devil pilot who says, 'The only woman who's ever loved me is my mother, and that's why I'm so free and easy when I climb into my crate.'

And yet *Dawn* is no Nazi film. This is particularly clear in the scene in which the U-boat commander's elderly mother refuses to participate in the small town's celebrations for her son's exploits, pointing out that the soldiers on the other side are also doing their duty and that one can't rejoice when other people are suffering. There is a similar scene in a Nazi film about three Merchant Navy cadets, Bernd Hofmann's *Fahrt ins Leben* (*Journey into Life*, 1940), which ends with an old woman soliloquising about the meaning of death, though in this case there is no compassion.

Siegfried Kracauer counts *Dawn* among the war films of the last years of the Weimar Republic 'which precisely through their impartiality elevate war to the rank of an unquestionable institution.'* In Kracauer's view, Hitler might have experienced a film like this – 'with its smell of real war' – as a lucky omen. Even if men like the U-boat commander did not join the Party, they were still destined to become Hitler's tools.

In 1930 the director of *Dawn*, Gustav Ucicky, had made *Das Flötenkonzert von Sanssouci* (*The Flute Concert at Sanssouci*), a film which presented Frederick the Great as an all-powerful patriarch and a leader of genius. In his 1931 film *Yorck*, Ucicky used the character of the Prussian general who rebels against his king to represent the true Prussian spirit. *Angriff*, Goebbels' Berlin-based National Socialist newspaper, wrote of the film: 'Today, in these similarly beleaguered times, Yorck and the Freiherr von und zum Stein are very close to us. His obedience was to the cause, not to the individual. And when he came into conflict with the individual, he decided in favour of the cause and became a rebel. If his brave deed had misfired, he would probably have been confined to a fortress for the rest of his life, or more probably would have lost his head. This strikes in us an uncommonly sympathetic note, and inspires a feeling almost of kinship with our own times, when every decent man is a rebel in spirit.'

Ucicky's first Third Reich film, *Flüchtlinge* (*Refugees*, 1933), was also the first film to receive Goebbels' annual state prize. Herbert Windt, who composed the music for *Dawn*, later worked on a whole series of Nazi films. In the very early days of the Third Reich it became obvious that the new

* *From Caligari to Hitler*, Princeton University Press, 1947

Dying for Germany: *Morgenrot*

authorities intended to reactivate the Prussian tradition whereby a soldier's life is the property of the king. As the U-boat commander in *Dawn* says at the moment of rescue: 'Our lives no longer belong to us. We sail on until the Lord God grants us leave.' This is a world where everyone is a soldier and his life is at the disposal of the state. The king is the embodiment of Prussia, as Hitler is of Germany. Honour is due to anyone who rebels against the decaying order of an existing society if at the same time it means paving the way for a new order based on the Führer principle.

In 1768, Frederick the Great wrote in his will: 'Discipline is based on obedience and orderliness. It begins with the general and ends with the drummer. Its foundation is submission. No subordinate has the right to object.' When the Nazis equated the Prussian spirit with National Socialism, they failed to acknowledge that in practice Prussian obedience was by no means as blind as Wolf Schneider's *The Soldiers' Book* suggests, and that in some respects the disciplinary measures employed by the Prussian army were by no means exclusively characteristic of the Prussians. The absurd lengths to which the notion of absolute obedience was carried in the Third Reich betrays the Nazis' fear of disorder, both in its outward manifestations – it was a

A leader of genius: *Das Flötenkonzert von Sanssouci*

spectre repeatedly invoked in accounts of the 1918–33 period, for example –
and on an ideological level.

Rudolf Hoess, later commandant of Auschwitz, was one of those who
returned disoriented from the First World War and joined a *Freikorps* unit so
that he could continue fighting in the Baltic, where he 'found himself at home
again, secure in the company of comrades'. For Hoess, who described himself
as 'a lone wolf who has to work out all his emotional experiences and
confusions for himself', membership first of a military unit, then of the
Freikorps, and finally of the SS, meant that he could hand over responsibility
for himself to a superior authority. And if this meant that personal and civic
ties were uprooted, the military code of ethics would take care of that. Hoess,
a failure in civilian life, became a political assassin during the Weimar
Republic, acting 'according to an unwritten law which, born of the exigencies
of the time, we made ourselves'. He saw himself as part of a community which
represented the nation's élite and whose *esprit de corps* 'nothing will break'.

In his first speech to the German Film Producers Association on 28 March
1933, Goebbels paid tribute to Luis Trenker's *The Rebel*, which had had its
first public showing a few weeks before the Nazi seizure of power. *The Rebel*

translated the conflict between Weimar and National Socialist politics into the time of the Tyrolean peasant rising against Napoleon's army of occupation. The film's hero takes part in the formation of a movement which corresponds to what in Nazi terminology was called the 'national uprising', and in whose illegal meetings the Nazi struggle against the Weimar government was romanticised. The rebel is also a prophet whose vision of a pan-German nation is projected on to the conflict between the Tyroleans and the Bavarians. The film's final scene was repeatedly copied during the Third Reich: the rebel is shot, but after his death he marches 'in spirit' within the ranks of the survivors and the newly recruited fighters.

Among the films which end on this note of apotheosis is *Hans Westmar* – about Horst Wessel – and *Hitlerjunge Quex* (*Hitler Youth Quex*). In the scene where the Nazi martyr Hans Westmar dies, death for Germany is for the first time equated with death for Hitler. A funeral oration for Hans proclaims: 'Raise the flag! And that means that the flag will rise again from death to the light of life, and with it his spirit will enter into us from the grave and march with us when one day we seize power for the glory and splendour of the new Reich!' Little Hitler Youth Quex is murdered by the Communists; he dies with the words of Baldur von Schirach's Hitler Youth marching song on his lips: 'Our flag flies before us...' The *Illustrierter Filmkurier* commented: 'The brave little soldier dies a hero's death, for his cause, for his comrades, for his beloved flag and for his Führer. But there are other German boys to lift high the flag which has been consecrated by the blood of one of the best.' Little Quex's death, with which thousands of Hitler Youth were to identify, takes its meaning from the words of the song which serves as a 'proud and triumphant' musical accompaniment to the film's last scene:

> Our flag flies before us.
> As one man we march into the future.
> For Hitler we march through night and through dread
> With the flag of youth for freedom and bread.
> Our flag flies before us, our flag is the new age.
> And the flag will lead us to eternity.
> Yes, the flag means more than death!

The 'die for Germany' theme finds recurring variations in Third Reich films. In the 1941 *Ich klage an* (*I accuse*) a major says that one has not only a duty but even a right to die for one's country. Death is the individual's sacrifice for the community, which in its various forms embodies the fatherland. Hitler had no need to be more explicit when in his speech to the Reichstag on 13 July 1934 he explained the justification for the executions following the alleged Röhm putsch. In the Third Reich, he said, 'there is only one embodiment of political power, and that is the National Socialist Party'. And the leader of this party was at the same time 'responsible for the destiny of the German nation and the supreme authority of the German people'.

A few weeks later, at the Nuremberg Rally, Hitler received this endorsement from his deputy Rudolf Hess: 'My Führer, you are Germany! When you act, the nation acts. When you judge, the people judge.' For the first time Hitler could greet the ranks of the faithful as Head of State, and enjoy his triumph over all those who had stood in his path to the summit of power. The only film in which Hitler played the leading part was the 'documentary record' of this Party Rally, whose title he chose himself: '*Triumph of the Will*, produced by the authority of the Führer, directed by Leni Riefenstahl.' In the film's prologue Hitler descends from the clouds like a Messiah to the masses awaiting salvation. His plane lands to the accompaniment of a bombastic commentary: 'On 5 September 1934, twenty years after the outbreak of the Great War, sixteen years after the beginning of the German people's humiliation, nineteen months after the German nation was reborn, Adolf Hitler was flying . . .'

The point was to show to Germany (which at first is seen only in hazy outline behind the clouds) 'the order, unity and determination of the National Socialist movement', as the *Völkischer Beobachter* for 1 September 1934 described the film's political mission. After the bloodbath of 30 June, the establishment of the SS as an autonomous organisation on 20 July, the death of Hindenburg on 2 August, and the referendum of 19 August which confirmed Hitler as 'Führer and Chancellor of the Reich', Head of State and Supreme Commander of the Army, it was essential to show the Party's strength to the people as a whole, and the means to this end was 'a documentary record of the unanimous loyalty to the Führer and so to Germany' which would be 'at the same time a resounding demonstration to the whole world of the peaceful intentions of the German people as embodied in the Führer'. The Nuremberg Rally was planned in concert with the film. In her book *Behind the Scenes of the Party Rally Film*, Leni Riefenstahl describes how 'to enable us to obtain novel visual effects, the city of Nuremberg gave its generous support in the building of bridges, towers and tracks, something which had never been possible before in the production of a film'. After 'arranging the most important details', Hitler went to Nuremberg himself 'to give the final instructions'.

The text of the film consists of policy speeches made by Hitler and his colleagues and oaths of loyalty from his fanatical supporters. The visual compositions, to a considerable extent modelled on Fritz Lang's monumental silent epic *The Nibelungen*, show Hitler as a new Siegfried and his supporters as extras in a colossal Wagner opera, an anonymous mass completely under

Triumph of the Will: the Pied Piper of Nuremberg

his sway. When the Labour Service parades, detachments of youth from every region stand ready 'to lead Germany into the new era'. In chorus they shout that 'though we have not been under heavy bombardment, we are still soldiers'. Time after time their God is revealed to them. The figure of Hitler is outlined in solitary glory against the sky. He dedicates the 'new military standards' by touching them with the so-called 'flag of blood'. By torchlight he commends the shining future of the nation he has united. He turns to 'his' comrades, 'his' youth. He poses as the prophet of a new religion, as the grand master of a mystical order, as an animal trainer who has disciplined his beasts of prey and is inspecting them before he lets them out into the world. The Pied Piper of Nuremberg — an intimidating spectacle for those who were still undecided on the sidelines, a beacon signalling Hitler's power beyond the frontiers of Germany, and a divine service for the faithful.

Again, in Leni Riefenstahl's two films on the Berlin Olympics, *Fest der Völker* (*Festival of Nations*) and *Fest der Schönheit* (*Festival of Beauty*), the Führer's presence lends a new dimension to the reality of the Third Reich. The athletes' performances are acts of worship in his honour. A bombastic prologue is meant to show how the Third Reich's ideal of beauty has its roots

Olympia: prototype for a warrior

in antiquity and how the training for war in Hitler's Germany reflects classical Greek ideals. The Third Reich is shown as heir to Sparta, and it is no accident that in the film's programme brochure the marathon is described as 'an epic hymn to endurance and the will to win'. Three years after the Olympics, the Führer was demanding of his people another kind of proof of 'endurance to the last breath' than the athletic exploits exalted in Leni Riefenstahl's rhythmic sequences. The reality of war was something Leni Riefenstahl cared not to endure: she worked briefly on reports from the front at the beginning of the war, but soon left to take refuge in the folk ballad ⁻ıysticism of her feature film *Tiefland* (1944). But her views of the Olympic fire bursting into flame and of Hitler's entry into the Olympic stadium were cited in *Wunschkonzert* (*Request Programme*), one of the most successful films of the Third Reich, as creating the right romantic atmosphere for young lovers on their first outing. And *Triumph of the Will* is repeatedly quoted in anti-Nazi films as a representative example of the process of transforming the individual into a soulless, anonymous part of the great mass, blindly following their Führer.

After *Triumph of the Will* there was no need to make another film about Hitler, and none was commissioned. He had been shown once and for all the way he wanted to be seen; and no actor was ever asked to represent him. Third Reich features occasionally have characters from German history or contemporary figures played in Hitler's image – but the parallel is always so obvious that the film has no need to emphasise the resemblance. A few words or a picture of Hitler on the wall are usually enough to remind people – if they need to be reminded at all – that the Führer is omnipresent in his Reich.

The following random examples will illustrate how Third Reich films treated this theme. *Refugees* (1933), the first film to receive the state prize, was named by Goebbels among those films which, though they may not have put the National Socialist programme into so many words, 'nevertheless contain the spirit of our spirit, the strength of our strength, the will of our will. Because of this the National Socialist state bestows on them a symbol of the honour due to them.' The film's theme is a representation of 'self-help and the Führer principle'.* The story, set on the Sino–Russian border in Manchuria in 1928, tells how a group of Volga German refugees persecuted by the Bolsheviks is rescued by a leader sent by destiny in the midst of their confusion and despair, 'a real man who turns his back on the effeminate November Germany, with its whining, its sycophancy and its petitioning, and passionately devotes himself to the true Germany'.† This hero, who is blond and athletic and thus embodies the Nazi racial ideal rather more accurately

---

* Oskar Kalbus: *Von Werden deutscher Filmkunst*, 1935.
† *ibid.*

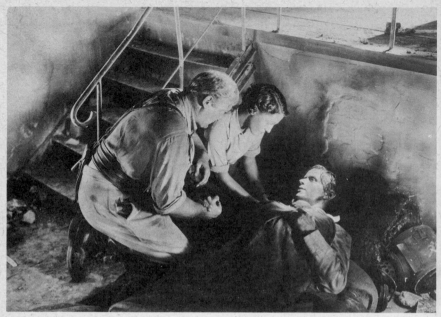

Dying for a cause: *Flüchtlinge*

than the actual 'Führer', disposes of those refugees he describes as 'miserable human material', and tells some others who won't come to heel immediately that they are chatterboxes; they must obey his orders because 'It's not your business to think.' This faculty is reserved for the leader. A boy who is absolutely devoted to him dies for the common interest; his last words are: 'I'm coming, Mother.' The leader comments: 'To die *for* something, that's the best thing there is. I wish I could die like that.' *Refugees* anticipates the return to the fatherland theme; and the transformation of a group of hopeless, quarrelling refugees into a community united by their leader's strength reflects an image of the German people which, in Third Reich terms, under Hitler's leadership placed its fate in his hands.

Karl Ritter's *Unternehmen Michael* (*Operation Michael*, 1937) tells the story of the spring offensive on the Western front in 1918. The film glorifies the capture of a pile of smoking ruins, once a French village, at the cost of thousands of lives. No one asks whether this offensive has any point. There is no mention of the fact that its objective – to prevent the French and British armies joining forces – was never achieved. Indeed, someone with no knowledge of German history might assume that Germany won the First World War. The commanding general is a father figure with unmistakable if only suggested echoes of Hindenburg. The hero of the story is a major with the general staff who leaves his post at headquarters to lead an assault unit and is killed in action. The last words spoken by the commanding general are directed to him: 'You know as well as I do that posterity will measure us not by the greatness of our victory but by the dimension of our sacrifice.' Major Zurlinden talks respectfully of his superior's responsibility ('giving orders, dispatching men on missions...'). The arguments against 'Operation Michael' are put into the mouth of a cavalry officer who plays the piano while the general is holding a conference to plan the offensive, and is told to stop playing by a staff officer (playing the piano is usually, though not always, considered unworthy of a real man in Nazi films). 'The gentlemen are working,' says the staff officer. The ensuing dialogue is characteristic:

CAVALRY OFFICER: Ah, I see. Music might weaken the impact of orders. Pity, I was hoping to comfort our distinguished staff in their anguish.
STAFF OFFICER: Major Zurlinden thinks the shortage of mortars will cost us a lot of blood.
CAVALRY OFFICER: Blood which would otherwise have been English.
STAFF OFFICER: What does the Captain mean by that?
CAVALRY OFFICER: When it's reason speaking, no one understands any more. We've been in the madhouse too long. Dare say once that men are slaughtering each other here for absolutely no reason, and people are flabbergasted.
OFFICER: That's obviously a civilian's way of looking at it. The captain must have picked it up on his last leave.
CAVALRY OFFICER: You don't need to go back to Germany to realise that what we're involved in here is totally senseless.
MAJOR: The unavoidable is never senseless, Wengern.
CAVALRY OFFICER: Is all this really unavoidable, Major?
MAJOR: How can we change it, may I ask?
CAVALRY OFFICER: Of course, the Major thinks it's impossible to make peace...
ANOTHER OFFICER: Make peace? That's really good. Try telling that to the English and the French!
CAVALRY OFFICER: As if they weren't fed up with it, too! The French wanted to go home eleven months ago.
MAJOR: But they didn't go home. When the ringleaders had been shot, they changed their minds.
CAVALRY OFFICER: So we go on killing each other?
MAJOR: There are 70 million of us. Those 70 million want to live, work, eat, drink. The world is big enough to make room for them. The world has got to understand that.

The story of *Urlaub auf Ehrenwort* (*Leave on Parole*, 1937), also directed by Karl Ritter, is set 'in the autumn of 1918, when the home front was already being undermined by pacifist slogans, while the field-grey lines, braving the superior forces of a whole world, unflinchingly stood their ground'. The film is a hymn to 'that damned sense of duty' which even Independent Social Democrat sympathisers consider more important than pacifist or socialist ideologies. *D III 88*, directed by Herbert Maisch in 1939, demonstrates how the 'spirit of the front-line pilots' in the First War was drummed into the Third Reich's Luftwaffe. The highest-ranking character says: 'There are personal differences everywhere, but in the service the only thing is the dedication of the whole person. Collaboration without friction, devotion without condition. This is the only way to make our service an instrument on which the Führer can rely absolutely in case of emergency.' Such an emergency is illustrated in the sequel to *D III 88*, Hans Bertram's *Kampfgeschwader Lützow* (*Battle Squadron Lützow*, 1941). This film takes up the *Dawn* theme of two comrades in love with the same girl. Grete writes NCO Paulsen a letter telling him that she does not love him, but the letter never reaches him. He is wounded in an air battle, 'but even as he dies he shows the spirit which inspires the Luftwaffe. With a last effort he brings his plane down and saves his comrades; then he collapses and dies. But his spirit lives on in hundreds, in thousands of men. And his sacrifice will never be forgotten' (*Illustrierter Filmkurier*). The film relieves the sadness of his death by sparing him the bitter truth of the letter.

Heroic death is glorified in other war films of 1941. In Herbert B. Fredersdorf's *Spähtrupp Hallgarten* (*Hallgarten Patrol*) the eulogy for the fallen mountain rifleman Hallgarten, and the resurrection of his spirit, resembles the last sequence of *Hitler Youth Quex*, except that this time the song is the Good Comrade Song: 'Our comrade Hallgarten was destined to fall in action. He has fulfilled his destiny as a good soldier. By giving up his life he has ennobled his soldier's spirit. He died so that our people might live. His soldier's deed will become part of the tradition of the mountain riflemen. It was an example of real, self-sacrificing comradeship.'

In Karl Ritter's *Stukas* (1941), there is a conversation between two officers on the Western Front during the Second War in which one of them says that 'death suddenly doesn't matter any more'. A man 'doesn't really think about his comrades' death any more, only about what they died for'. Hölderlin is quoted:

> O take me, take me into your ranks,
> That I will not die a common death!
> To die in vain, I crave not that, but
> Only to fall on the hill of sacrifice.
>
> For the Fatherland, to bleed the heart's blood . . .
> Now heralds of victory descend, the battle

> Is ours! Live on high, o Fatherland,
> And count not the dead! For you,
> Beloved, not one too many is fallen.

Himmelhunde (*Sky Dogs*, 1942), directed by Roger von Norman — a film which was clearly aimed at young people — takes the enthusiasm of young glider pilots and steers it on to a military course. The conflict between discipline and comradeship is resolved thus: 'Orders are above those who receive them and those who give them.' And: 'We've no use for scabs who always think of themselves first and question the reason for an order instead of simply carrying it out.' Third Reich cinema produced its noblest hero's death in loyal performance of duty in Eduard von Borsody's 1940 film *Wunschkonzert* (*Request Programme*). Here, on the Western front in 1940, a musician guides his straggling comrades back to their original position — a church — by playing the organ, for which he pays with his life. This noble death, heralded by music played without a single wrong note, was needless to say a world apart from the reality of the front-line.

3. Brown or Red?

On 23 March 1933, Hitler announced in his government policy declaration: 'In conjunction with the political decontamination of our public life, the government will embark on a systematic campaign to restore the nation's moral health. The whole educational system, theatre, film, literature, the press and broadcasting – all of them will be means to this end ... They will all be harnessed to help preserve the eternal values which are part of the essential nature of our people.'

On 10 May 1933, Goebbels announced in the *Völkischer Beobachter* that it was his Ministry's task 'to put Germany into a state of spiritual mobilisation. The Ministry has thus the same function in the area of spiritual matters as the War Ministry has in the field of armaments...' At the inauguration of the Chamber of Culture on 15 November 1933, Goebbels announced, 'What we want is more than a dramatisation of the Party's programme.' His ideal was 'a profound marriage of the spiritual nature of the heroic concept of life with the eternal laws of art'. This explains why there are only a few feature films whose main object is to glorify the Party. National Socialism was to find expression not in the choice of subject but in the way the subject was handled. It is only at the beginning of the Third Reich that there are films wholly devoted to 'heroism in the Party and the movement'. Goebbels was dissatisfied with the first two of these – Franz Seitz's *SA Man*

Brand and Franz Wenzler's *Hans Westmar*, both made in 1933. The first adaptation of Hanns Heinz Ewers' novel *Horst Wessel* (the film was also called *Horst Wessel* – the final version became *Hans Westmar*) was banned by Goebbels on the grounds that 'National Socialism can under no circumstances be a licence for artistic failure. On the contrary, the greater the idea to be expressed, the higher the demands made on the artist'. Goebbels saw 'no particular value in having our stormtroopers march about on stage or screen. Their place is on the street. But if one is going to try to solve National Socialist problems artistically, one must be aware of the fact that in art, as in other things, it is not a question of wanting to but of knowing how. However spectacularly staged, a National Socialist message is far from being a substitute for real artistic deficiency. The National Socialist government has never issued an order for stormtrooper films to be made. On the contrary, it would regard an excess of them as dangerous.'

Looking at them in a contemporary light, one can detect in films like *Hans Westmar* (subtitled 'One of the many') and Hans Steinhoff's *Hitler Youth Quex* (subtitled 'A film about German youth and its spirit of sacrifice'), as well as their panegyrics to the 'martyred young warriors', a caricature of the Communist adversary which does not preclude a kind of flirtation with this very enemy. Evidently, though Communism was seen as the most dangerous of opponents, the individual Communist was a potential Party member. In *Hans Westmar* three kinds of Communists are juxtaposed. There is the party boss who exploits misery and transmits the Moscow line. There is the small-time official, with Jewish characteristics, who incites a mass meeting against 'Popish priests, socialist sheep, and that miserable pack of brownshirts financed by heavy industry', and who warns the 'Nazi hooligans' that the streets belong to the Communists. When a fight breaks out in a meeting hall, he crawls under the speaker's table; and of course he and a woman colleague, who also looks Jewish, are held directly responsible for the hero Hans Westmar's murder. But there is also Ross, the Communist idealist, who tells Westmar that only a proletarian can understand the proletariat. In the film's last scene, the torchlight procession of the SA on the eve of the Nazi seizure of power, his clenched fist opens into a Nazi salute.

Heini Völker, alias Hitler Youth Quex, is the son of a Communist father who under the threat of a beating forces him to bellow the 'Internationale'. Heini's father is violent and usually drunk, but the film allows him some sympathy. He too has seen better days. He is a Communist because the proletariat has to fight for its life if it is not to be permanently on the dole. Stoppel, who invites Heini on a Communist Youth outing and who organises a raid on the Hitler Youth hostel, may say that his little Hitler Youth friend has to be eliminated; but when the Communist raiding party has been alerted and sets off to liquidate Heini, Stoppel gives them no help. The example of the Hitler Youth seems to have made the same impression on him as Westmar's courage did on Ross in *Hans Westmar*. In the end it is a totally uncommitted baker who zealously betrays Heini — a non-political German who aligns himself with the stronger party in the political power struggle.

This flirtation with the enemy is also apparent in certain scenes in *Hitler Youth Quex* which reveal conscious echoes of leftwing film classics. When mother Völker turns on the gas tap to join her son in death, one is reminded of the death of the heroine in *Mother Krausen's Journey to Happiness.** In both films the portrait of social misery is the same. The first scene in *Hitler Youth Quex*, in which a boy steals an apple, gets his ears boxed by the greengrocer, and triggers off a Communist demonstration in front of the shop, is influenced by films like *Kuhle Wampe*. The film's ballad singer comes from *The Threepenny Opera*. And in the final scene there are unmistakable echoes of Lang's *M*.

Both *Hans Westmar* and *Hitler Youth Quex* illustrate the way in which Nazi film propaganda represented the struggle for the German soul between National Socialism and Communism. This is how Hans Westmar views a Communist street demonstration: 'I'm telling you, what's going on down there is about the whole of Germany. In the streets. And that's why we must get to the people. We can't stand aside any more. It's all or nothing. We must fight, side by side with the workers!' To the objection that the workers want nothing to do with Nazi students because they are from a completely different class, Westmar has an answer ready: 'We simply can't talk about classes any longer. We are also workers, we work with our heads — and our place is next to our brother who works with his hands.'

The key scene in *Hitler Youth Quex* is a conversation in which the Hitler Youth brigade leader and the Communist father fight for the young hero's mind. Heini, of course, as the embodiment of an ailing Germany, listens in silence to this tug-of-war for his mind, until the brigade leader's words give him a new resolution:

BRIGADE LEADER: Hello, Heini. The doctor says you can go out again if you feel like it.
HEINI: Where should I go?
FATHER: What a question! With your father, of course. That's where you belong.
BRIGADE LEADER: But that's precisely the question. Where does the boy belong today? Look, I had very good parents. But when I was fifteen, I ran away. Wanted to go to sea, be a cabin boy. Somewhere I knew there were islands, with palm trees. Africa! Thousands of boys ran away.

* *Mutter Krausens Fahrt ins Glück*, directed by Piel Jutzi in 1929, one of the most celebrated of the German realist films of the late Twenties.

'Where does the boy belong today?': brigade leader, Hitler Youth and Communist father in *Hitlerjunge Quex*

FATHER: Little devils, that's what they were.

BRIGADE LEADER: Ah, but you know, boys are marvellous. There's a big mystery in boys. Always has been. They ran away to join the fur traders, the gipsies. One day they all get bitten by the bug. Then they start to roam. Where does a boy belong? Well, why don't you ask your own boy?

FATHER: Come on then, say something.

BRIGADE LEADER: Well, I don't know whether you were in the war, but . . .

FATHER: Oh, and how . . .

BRIGADE LEADER: Two million boys volunteered in those days. All sons of fathers, all had a mother. And where did they belong?

FATHER: I'm a simple man. I'm a man of the people.

BRIGADE LEADER: You've heard of the movement, haven't you?

FATHER: Movement! Up, one, two, up, one, two – that was my movement. Until a bullet got me. Then I was put in plaster. Then there was more movement – stretch your limbs, bend, straight, bend, straight – then I limped to the labour exchange. Week after week, year after year. That was my movement. Nothing else ever moved me. I went to pieces! D'you think I got fat from eating too much? No, it was because I was out of work. Sitting around made me fat. So where do I belong? I belong with my mates, from my own class. And where I belong, the boy belongs too.

BRIGADE LEADER: To your own class? You mean, with the Internationale? Eh?
FATHER: Yes, of course, the Internationale.
BRIGADE LEADER: Hm. Where were you born?
FATHER: In Berlin . . .
BRIGADE LEADER: And where's that?
FATHER: On the Spree.
BRIGADE LEADER: On the Spree — yes, of course. But where? What country?
FATHER: Oh, come on! In Germany, of course.
BRIGADE LEADER: Yes, of course, in Germany — in our Germany. Now you think about that.

This scene does not appear in Karl Aloys Schenzinger's novel *Hitler Youth Quex*, which had been published in 1932. But the book does contain the incident of the Communist Youth outing where Heini is put off by the wild goings-on of his friends and sneaks off into the woods. There he notices in the distance the light from a Hitler Youth camp-fire, marches towards it through the darkness, and 'with heart pounding' watches from his hiding-place as the Hitler Youth, in formation, listen to their brigade leader.

He was probably making a real speech. Heini could only make out a few words; he heard 'movement' and 'Führer', he picked up half a sentence — '. . . each his life for another.' While he was listening, already wondering whether he should creep up a little nearer so that he could follow more of it, he got a tremendous fright. *'Deutschland, Deutschland, über alles . . .'* A thousand voices swept over him like a warm wave. 'I'm a German, too,' he thought, and this awareness came to him with such unexpected force that it was like nothing he had ever known in his life, at school, at home, or in front of Parliament when the soldiers presented arms. He wanted to join in the singing, but his voice failed him. This was German soil, German woods, these were German boys; and he realised that he was standing apart, alone, without support, and he did not know what to do with these sudden overwhelming emotions.

The uniform represents for the boy the realisation of his dream of belonging to this community, this élite of youth. The Hitler Youth hostel replaces his family, and discipline allows him to forget his private drama. 'Anyone wearing this uniform has to obey orders.' When the brigade leader tells Quex ('lively as quicksilver') that he is not to distribute Nazi election pamphlets in the 'reddest district', the 'Beusselkietz', because it could be dangerous, the boy shouts back: 'When you were an officer in the field, did you stop your soldiers advancing if there was shooting?' At which the leader lets him go, 'in God's name'.

In an analysis of the film *Hitler Youth Quex* which appears in *The Study of Culture at a Distance*,* edited by Margaret Mead and Rhoda Métraux, Gregory Bateson remarks that the characterisation of Communists in the film

* Chicago, 1953

38

Communist demonstration in *Hans Westmar*

is a Nazi self-portrait. It reveals what in their own view the Nazis would be like without their discipline, or in other words what they are really like beneath the veneer of discipline. To illustrate this argument, Bateson quotes a scene in which a Young Communist at the station tries to provoke a group of Hitler Youth lined up in front of their brigade leader by throwing a half-eaten apple into a Hitler Youth's face. Only the brigade leader's call for order prevents the Hitler Youth from turning into the kind of rabble represented by the Young Communists in the same scene. When a fight threatens to break out in the Hitler Youth hostel after Heini has been called by his nickname 'Quex' by another boy, chaos is again only forestalled by an order from a superior. The 'thigh-slapping' during the outing, which is intended to characterise the Communists as a sadistic, undisciplined rabble, was in fact often practised by the Hitler Youth. The Communists are presented as the antitype of the National Socialist ideal, which means that the attributes they are given have their psychological roots in the Nazi character. Bateson illustrates this by contrasting various characters: the brigade leader and the Völker father; Hitler Youth Quex and Grundler, who is unequal to the demands made on a Hitler Youth; and Ulla, of the League of German Women, and the Communist vamp Gerda.

A similar parallel between Nazism and Communism can be traced in *Hans*

Red Army soldiers and Volga Germans in *Friesennot*

Westmar. The extent to which the caricature of Communists reflects the Nazi mentality can be seen in the way the Communists in the film behave among themselves. Is it a coincidence that the leader of the Communist conspiracy refers to 'the average German' with the same contemptuous smile as Bismarck in a Nazi historical film made seven years after *Hans Westmar*? The slogan used in the Communist demonstration in *Hans Westmar* – 'Nazis, drop dead!' – is modelled on the Nazi slogan, 'Jews, drop dead!'

The feud with Communism is also the subject of Hans Zöberlein's *Um das Menschenrecht* (*For the Rights of Man*, 1934), in which homage is paid to the *Freikorps* as the effective bulwark against Bolshevism. Four war veterans are contrasted: 'The artist pursues the idea of world revolution. The second soldier sees his family starving and joins the ranks of the red proletariat. The third goes back to his farm discontented. The fourth, once a student, joins the *Freikorps*. All four of them have lost faith in their country. All around Communism is lurking, intent on doping and then enslaving the weak-minded.'*

In *Friesennot* (*Frisians in Peril*, 1935), directed by Peter Hagen (i.e. state

* Kalbus, *op. cit.*

script adviser Willi Krause), and distributed by the National Socialist State Propaganda Directorate, Department of Film, the anti-Communist propaganda is focused on a Volga German village. Red Army soldiers are levying taxes and duties in the name of the new Communist authorities, and making life as difficult as they can for the Frisians. Open fighting breaks out between the Bolsheviks and the Volga Germans when Mette, daughter of a Frisian and a Russian woman, becomes the girl-friend of the Russian commissar; whereupon the Frisians throw her into the swamp. The film ends with a bloodbath in which all the Red Army soldiers are killed. The Frisians set fire to their village and leave to find a new home.

A contemporary audience would laugh at the scene in which one of the Volga Germans says that Mette cannot throw herself at a foreigner because though her mother may have been a Russian, her father was 'a Frisian, and our blood weighs more than foreign blood'. Looked at today, the film's portrait of Commissar Chernov seems a surprising deviation from the brutal murderers of *Refugees*, *Comrades at Sea* and *GPU*. Commissar Chernov tells his girl-friend: 'I had no one any more who loved me or whom I could love. So I went on living without questioning my conscience or·my heart. Now I've found you, and if you'll come with me – I am due to be relieved in a few weeks – it will be easy for us to find a way of escaping.' Only after this dream has been shattered by Mette's death does he give his soldiers a free hand.

Typical of the cynicism of Nazi anti-Communist propaganda is a conversation between the Commissar and the village elder. For the Party which fought against the Church, threw priests into concentration camps, and abused the ordinary German citizen's trust in its authority, Communism is the anti-Christ. The village elder comes to see the Commissar. In the outside office he notices obscene, anti-religious pictures, and on the Commissar's office door – in *four* languages (just who in this Volga village is supposed to speak French or English?) – an inscription which reads 'There is no God.' The conversation between the two men is as follows:

WAGNER: You didn't tell me the truth! Those pictures outside, what are they for?
CHERNOV: I did tell you the truth. What's it got to do with the pictures my men put there?
WAGNER: That's blasphemy!
CHERNOV: There's no God in Russia.
WAGNER: So, there's no God in Russia. Who says so? Who abolished him then?
CHERNOV: The authorities.
WAGNER: All authority comes from God. How can you abolish God?

In another scene there is a modification in the treatment of the theme of God-given authority in the Soviet Union – which could be read as the ordinary German's heart-felt hope about the Third Reich régime: 'All

Varieties of Russian to suit the time: *The Postmaster* (Hilde Krahl, Heinrich George) . . .

government, good or evil, comes from God. Let us pray that He has given us a good one.'

Frisians in Peril was banned in 1939 following the Hitler–Stalin non-aggression pact; then in 1941, after the invasion of Russia, it was re-released with the title *Red Storm over the Village*. Veit Harlan's 1937 film *Mein Sohn, der Herr Minister* (*My Son, the Minister*), a coarsened adaptation of a French comedy refurbished in Nazi style, equated parliamentary government with Communism. Set during the time of the Popular Front in France, the film has the Communist agitator as the man who pulls the strings behind the democratic curtain. In a style modelled on *Hans Westmar*, this 'friend of the people' opens a Party election meeting with the words, 'Comrades, I am the ears of France which listen for you. I am the eyes of France which see for you.'

In the 1938 film *Comrades at Sea*, directed by Heinz Paul, the Spanish civil war is presented as a Communist uprising against the legal government of the country. A German passenger ship is commandeered in Spanish waters by sinister Communists – who immediately kill the captain – and only rescued by the intervention of the German navy. This film apart, the only other reference to the Spanish civil war in Third Reich feature films is

... and *Kadetten*, after the invasion of Russia

incidental − just one of many adventures in an officer's career. Shooting on Karl Ritter's *Condor Legion*, about the part played by German troops in Spain between 1936 and 1938, began on 9 August 1939 only to be brought to a halt on 1 September 'owing to the outbreak of war and the fact that the Luftwaffe was needed for it'.*

After the Nazi–Soviet non-aggression pact, anti-Communist caricatures disappeared. Gustav Ucicky's 1940 film *The Postmaster* presents the Russians in a sympathetic light; and in the same year Wolfgang Liebeneiner's *Bismarck* has Bismarck tell Wilhelm I that the military pact with Russia will safeguard the Prussians on their Eastern flank. When the King objects that this is a new and disturbing departure and the newspapers will all side with the Poles, Bismarck counters: 'By the time the moaners decide to do something about it, we will be mobilised. They sharpen their tongues and shoot with paper. We sharpen our sabres and we'll shoot with needle guns.'

A year later the situation was reversed. Initially, the invasion of Russia is justified only in films in which war is made to seem necessary because of 'the

* Alfred Bauer, *Deutscher Spielfilmalmanach 1929–1950*. Another *Condor Legion*, assembled from newsreel material by Fritz Hippler, was released later in 1939.

Russian as murderer in *GPU* (Andrews Engelman)

nameless sufferings of the German people in Poland', thus by-passing the fact that Hitler considered a clash with Russia inevitable. The 'sub-human' Slav in Karl Ritter's *Cadets* (1941) has Russian features but is no Communist. Only *GPU* (1942), also directed by Karl Ritter, is a directly anti-Communist propaganda film. The heroine of this clumsy melodrama is a Baltic German who, after seeing her whole family shot by a GPU (Russian secret police) agent when she was a child, joins the GPU herself in order to trace and eliminate the murderer. She stands between two worlds, one of them peopled by black-hearted Communist barbarians, the other represented by a pair of lovers persecuted by the GPU. These two are of course unable to fight the GPU and win. After avenging the murder of her family, Olga Feodorovna commits suicide: 'One must have the chance to die for something – I cannot live.'

The version of the film which I have seen ends here. The *Illustrierter Filmkurier* refers to a final scene in which the lovers are saved from torture at the Soviet trade mission in Rotterdam by the German invasion of Holland, and set off to find a new life for themselves. The film fabricates clichés which are so simplistic, crude and spurious that the propaganda loses all credibility.

Soviet agents dance the foxtrot in tails; the dialogue includes sentences like 'England will never allow the subjugation of Poland'; there is a story about someone who made a career for himself 'without being either a Jew or a proletarian.' The GPU torturers are so crudely 'subhuman' and criminally inspired that no audience could believe that the young student who falls into their clutches would take them for genuine policemen. Characteristically, the film makes no attempt to differentiate its Russian characters; only German soldiers, advancing to their Führer's orders, can liberate the imprisoned lovers.

4. 'Führer, command — we will obey'

On 10 November 1938, Hitler addressed the German press. The speech was made in private, but a recording of it was issued after the war. Although he spoke on the day after the *Kristallnacht*, Hitler made no mention of the persecution of the Jews. The purpose of the speech was to convey official thanks to the press for their propaganda efforts during the Munich crisis. After a digression on his victories, Hitler moved on to attack the intellectuals, whose attitudes were already causing him concern even at this time of success — 'And what would they be like if we were to have a failure for once?' This brought Hitler to his main theme. The German people, he said, must 'learn to be so fanatical in their belief in final victory that even if we suffer an occasional reverse, the nation will interpret it on, so to speak, a higher plane: this will blow over, and in the end victory will be ours . . . To achieve this, it is essential for the press in particular to be totally committed to the principle: the leadership is doing the right thing. In other words, it is essential — without in any way discounting or debating the possibility of mistakes — that the fundamental rightness of the leadership is repeatedly emphasised. This is the crucial point. It is particularly essential, you see, from the point of view of the people. I am often asked, even now — this is liberal backsliding — this question: Yes, but shouldn't one leave it to the people for once? Well, gentlemen, you know I flatter myself that I have accomplished a few things — more, at any rate, than many a cobbler or cowgirl.'

Work in progress: Hitler and Goebbels at the Ufa studios

Long before this speech, Hitler's demand that the German people should be educated in an 'absolute, obdurate, self-evident and unwavering conviction' ('In the end we shall achieve all that is necessary') had been put into action. His order that there should be an unceasing 'appeal to the nation's strength' and to the readiness of the masses to expect miracles from their Führer and to submit unconditionally to his will, was a permanent theme in Third Reich films. Goebbels had already stated, in a speech to theatre managers on 8 May 1933, that 'the essence of any propaganda is to win people over to an idea which is so profound and so vital that in the end they fall under its spell and cannot escape from it.'

On 9 February 1934, Goebbels told the State Film Organisation that he was convinced that 'film is one of the most modern and far-reaching ways of influencing the masses today'. Anything that stood in the way of this persuasion technique had to be removed. Criticism was incompatible with the Führer principle and was therefore abolished. As Wilhelm Weiss* put it in an article called 'A Critique of Criticism' (*Deutsche Presse*, No. 51/52, 21

* Head of the Reich Press Association and editor of the *Völkischer Beobachter*, the leading Party newspaper.

All-powerful leader: Emil Jannings as *Der Herrscher*

December 1935): 'The critic of today is no longer a private individual who arbitrarily determines his attitude to art according to some personal or other point of view; today's critic has a public duty assigned to him by the National Socialist state and the National Socialist ideology.' In the *Völkischer Beobachter* of 29 November 1936, Alfred-Ingemar Berndt wrote of the critic's transformation from 'arts critic to servant of the arts'. Appraisal of the arts should include 'all there is to be said, but should not evaluate. The only possible standard for judging a work of art in the National Socialist state is the National Socialist concept of culture. Only the party and the state are in a position to determine standards according to this National Socialist concept of culture.'

It is thus hardly surprising that Goebbels was contemptuous of the idea of freedom of expression. As an example of his attitude, Helmut Heiber quotes the argument Goebbels used in February 1939 'to justify his decree which was intended to protect the "hallowed reserves of our political and ideological life" from what he termed "the muck of the streets"'. With a logic peculiar to himself, Goebbels wrote: 'Freedom of expression or no freedom of expression, the Führer has still in the past year brought back ten million Germans to the Reich. And that is surely something.'* (For Hitler, as we have seen, this argument was insufficient. He had asked on 10 November 1938 how this 'chicken-hearted people' would behave if there were no more successes of 'world historical importance' to be recorded.)

The Führer principle anticipated a loyalty whose reward was to be the promised final victory. On the other hand, 'Loyalty is its own reward, and so is disloyalty.' Thus privy councillor Clausen in Veit Harlan's film *Der Herrscher* (*The Ruler*, 1937). The mild-mannered art collector of Gerhart Hauptmann's play *Before Sunset* here becomes a powerful leader, the 'first worker' of the Clausen works, as Hitler was the 'first worker of the state'. Sitting below a portrait of the Führer on the wall during a board meeting, he thunders: 'We exist to provide work and bread for millions and millions of people. We exist to work for the community. To serve the community must be the aim of every industrialist who is aware of his responsibilities. What I am suggesting is the first commandment in my factory. Everything else must be subordinated to this, even if it means the whole place going under with me. If anyone refuses to obey this supreme commandment, there's no place for him at the Clausen works.' Whereas in Hauptmann's play Clausen goes to pieces over the conflict between his love for a young girl and the intransigence of his children, the 'ruler' of the film renounces his family. 'Prevailed upon by the responsibility I have for the factory I have been building for generations,' he disinherits his family and bequeathes the Clausen works to 'the state, that is

* *Joseph Goebbels*, Berlin, 1962.

Nazi Cinema

the community. I am certain that from the ranks of my workers and employees, who helped me build this factory, there will rise a man who is called upon to continue my work. No matter whether he comes from the furnace or the drawing-board, the laboratory or the work-bench, I will teach him the few things a man who is leaving can teach a new man. A born leader needs no teacher to guide his genius.'

The 'ruler' was played by Emil Jannings, who as Friedrich Wilhelm I in Hans Steinhoff's *Der alte und der junge König* (*The old King and the young King*, 1935) had already had to invoke the supreme authority of the state in words taken from Nazi vocabulary. The first opening of parliament in the Third Reich was held at the garrison church in Potsdam, so as to make National Socialism appear as the restoration of the Prussian tradition. When the Prussian king has Lieutenant Katte beheaded, though the court has merely sentenced him to be confined, he is acting as the 'supreme judicial authority', like Hitler after the alleged Röhm putsch. 'His will is law, and if there is any opposition to him he must eliminate it.' Critics are silenced by a very simple method: 'These matters are too important to be understood by such small minds.'

It was Nazi propaganda's constant endeavour to demonstrate that the Führer's will is law because he embodies the people. In this world, however, democratic institutions do not express popular opinion. 'The Press is not the people,' Bismarck reminds his King in Wolfgang Liebeneiner's *Bismarck* (1940). In Herbert Selpin's *Carl Peters* (1941), the colonial pioneer Peters refuses to justify himself to a parliamentary committee: 'What I have done I will answer for to myself. And to Germany.' When a member of the committee quite reasonably objects, 'We are Germany, because we are the people,' his words are discredited because they are spoken by a Jewish member of parliament; and with heavy irony the blond superman replies: 'So, *you* are the people! You must excuse me – I could never of course have suspected that.'

In Veit Harlan's *My Son, the Minister* (1937), the idea of freedom as 'democracy's most sacred possession' is ridiculed because it is misused by a Communist in an unctuous propaganda speech. The mechanics of parliamentary government are mocked in a conversation between the outgoing and the incoming Minister in which, between the lines, the inefficacy of a parliamentary 'gossip club' is contrasted with the Third Reich's 'abolition' of unemployment.

'Minister, I wish to follow an honourable custom of this House and bid farewell to you as the departing Minister.'

'And I should like to follow an honourable custom of this House and, as they say, hand over to you, as the incoming Minister, my desk.'

'I am sorry, Minister, that you are leaving.'

'Ha, you mean because you are displacing me. Aha, my dear fellow, that is the fate of every Minister who swims in parliamentary waters.'

'Parliamentary government is the noblest institution that democracy has produced.'

'Bravo, bravo. That has a delightful ring to it. I've said it myself at least three times in every election speech. But, frankly, neither of us really believes it.'

'It is very important to me to raise the living standards of this country.'

'But my dear sir, that happens automatically. If things go on as they are, in no time at all everyone in France will have been a Minister. For which he will afterwards receive a pension of 50,000 francs and live happily ever after. What more do you want?'

'You're very ironical.'

'On the contrary, I'm only being honest. Now that I'm no longer a Minister, I can after all afford to be honest.'

'I see my most important duty as being to reduce unemployment. Because, frankly, so far there really hasn't been enough done in this field.'

'I beg your pardon — the House has been permanently occupied with the question of unemployment. We have formed seven commissions and set up six committees. I myself have made at least thirty speeches on unemployment. Even with the best will in the world could one really do more? If the number of unemployed has risen in spite of that, well, God help us, what can we do about it? You won't be able to do very much to alter the situation either, young man. Well, now, to work again. I wish you better luck than I had, and don't overwork yourself!'

'I consider myself responsible to Parliament, to my constituents, and above all to the people.'

'Responsible! That's whimsy. What can happen to us, after all? Face to face with nothing — with a pension of 50,000 francs. Come on now, that's surely something that can be endured? But you have work to do. Sincerely, I wish you all the best.'

In spite of this contempt for democratic institutions, Nazi propaganda was constantly at odds with the Weimar Republic, and never tired in its efforts to demonstrate the necessity of the Führer principle and of the Nazi seizure of power for the salvation of the German people. In a 1937 Hans Steinhoff film version of Ibsen's *An Enemy of the People*, the eponymous hero is intended to represent the notion of the individual's sacrifice for the well-being of the community. He is defeated in his fight against the 'solid liberal majority', in spite of his visionary scheme for a life of freedom and beauty. True to the spirit of Nazi ideology, the film changes the play by having Dr Stockmann, a physician in a small German spa during the Weimar Republic, take up his position again after the Nazi seizure of power and implement his reform programme. This time the majority is on his side.

Nazi films portray the November revolution entirely from the war veteran's point of view. In Herbert Maisch's *D III 88* (1939), a pilot officer, hearing that revolution has broken out at home, refuses to go on fighting

Rearmament endorsed in *Pour le Mérite*

'while back home they're behaving like pigs'. He has no intention of 'getting killed at the eleventh hour for a country which will just laugh at us'. In Karl Ritter's *Pour le Mérite* (1938), a war veteran tells a Weimar Republic court: 'I have nothing whatsoever in common with this country, because I hate democracy like the plague. Whatever you may do, I will try to disrupt and destroy it wherever I can. We must put back on its feet a Germany which represents the ideals of the soldier at the front. I consider it my duty in life to help achieve this. And I shall go about it as a soldier would.'

Pour le Mérite enthusiastically endorses the illegal German rearmament, and gloatingly reveals how men who represent the old army make fools of the parliamentary control commissions. One of them explains his motive: 'I serve a government which I know is ruining Germany. But it will not be allowed to do this.' The Major in this scene takes it for granted that a parliamentary government will mean Germany's downfall, and will consequently prepare the way for the Nazi party: 'There will have to be a miracle! If I didn't believe in this miracle, I wouldn't be here. Moreover we are not alone. There are other men, better men than us, who believe in this miracle and are fighting to see it happen.'

This is not the only film to show the Weimar Republic as a quagmire in which no decent person could survive. There is a longing to escape into the country and the fresh air of the woods, away from the desolation of the cities where, if one were to believe Nazi films, Jewish intellectuals, black jazz trumpeters and Communist scum rule the roost. This was the world which the blond hero of *Fugitives* fled for those distant lands where there was still a need for real men. In this German Babylon of the Twenties the Party emerges in Nazi films as a secret order. In *Pour le Mérite* two war veterans meet by chance on the street and discover that they are both wearing the Party badge under their lapels. In Hans H. Zerlett's *Venus vor Gericht* (*Venus on Trial*, 1941), a Nazi sculptor, who is of course doing badly in this era of decadent art and Jewish art critics, receives a visit from the bailiff. Finding a swastika flag in the studio, the bailiff leaves without requisitioning anything; and as he does so, he smiles and raises his arm in a Nazi salute.

Pour le Mérite concludes with the announcement of general conscription on 16 March 1935. As the exultant masses converge on the war memorials of the First War, Goebbels can be heard reading the text of the law which established the Wehrmacht. The veteran soldiers are wearing new uniforms, and the engines of the Third Reich's first fighter squadron start up 'the epic song of the spirit of "Pour le Mérite"'.

A few days after the introduction of general conscription, a film called *Hundert Tage* (*A Hundred Days*) – a German–Italian co-production directed by Franz Wenzler from the play of the same name by Benito Mussolini and Giovacchino Forzano – had its first German showing. Here, Napoleon serves as a projection of the Fascist dictators, and uncannily he also anticipates their destiny. He leaves Elba to rejoin the path 'which destiny has allotted me. If I had been victorious at Moscow, my dream would have been fulfilled – a united Europe, an eternal peace after so many wars. Mother, I must take up the fight again. If I succeed in uniting Europe, my name will live as long as the Immortals.' Like all mothers in Nazi films, Napoleon's mother agrees with her son.

Mussolini's Napoleon also considers himself responsible only to the people. He never wanted war, but has always 'had to fight for everything . . . I stretched out my hand in peace to the sovereigns of Europe – and they say my assassination would be an act of humanity.' Mussolini's Napoleon also rejects the notion that the French Parliament represents France. Enthusiastic workers, artisans and soldiers 'and the woman I took to be a petitioner and who then offered me her savings – that is the country, Fouché, not your five hundred speechifiers in Parliament – I could chase them from the House with four grenadiers at any time'. After the battle of Waterloo, ingeniously planned by Napoleon but lost through the incompetence of an old

A man of destiny: Werner Krauss as Napoleon in *Hundert Tage*

general, he asks this very parliament which he so disdains to grant him 'extraordinary powers of absolute rule for a fixed period for the purpose of saving the nation'. Like Hitler, this Napoleon demands loyalty in return for loyalty. Forced to abdicate, he remarks: 'Rivers of blood have been shed. I have allowed a whole generation to be killed, and I will not shirk the responsibility for this. I saw it as a sacred mission to break up these ludicrous little states of Europe, to demolish the arbitrary and meaningless frontiers and customs barriers, and to bring all nations together in one great community. Every nation as an active member of one great, united country, no more war in Europe – that was my dream, and that is my political testament.'

Napoleon's deposition is represented as a cautionary tale. He might have turned defeat into victory. Parliament has nothing to gain by keeping its distance from him. The House dispatches five of its members to the victorious Blücher, who himself sends only one emissary to dictate his armistice conditions. Humiliated, these intermediaries are cynically made aware of their impotence: 'Be as indignant as you like. Bring your army out against us, if you have one.' At this moment what France lacks is a man of destiny who knows how to apply the politics of strength. There is no need to add that in Nazi Germany and Fascist Italy such men were fortunately in control.

Third Reich films did not venture to ask what might happen if success eluded these leaders. Such a question was inadmissible. What was not allowed to happen simply could not happen.

5. And Tomorrow the Whole World

Third Reich literature and film are always presenting their heroes with an all or nothing choice. If you don't accept the challenge, you are a weakling. If you doubt that under Adolf Hitler's leadership 'all' will be won, you can't be admitted to the ranks of the faithful. The Führer tolerates no other god but himself. 'At this hour when the earth is consecrating itself to the sun, we have only one thought. Our sun is Adolf Hitler.'* Readiness to obey orders is the 'birthright' of a youth drilled for battle: 'I heard not a single song expressing any tender emotion of friendship, love for fellow-man, joy of living, hope for future life.'† War means embarking on an adventure, an irresistible advance; and if that means turning flourishing towns into smouldering ruins, the blame rests with those who refuse to submit to the Führer.

> We shall go on marching
> Though everything falls apart.
> For Germany is ours today,
> And tomorrow the whole world.

Even though the 'greatest commander of all time' announced his plans for territorial acquisition early enough for the opposition to fight the Nazis —

* From *Childhood and Society* by Erik H. Erikson, originally quoted from *Education for Death*, G. Ziemer, Oxford University Press, 1941.
† *ibid.*

even before the seizure of power — with the slogan 'Hitler means war', Hitler avoided all responsibility for the war. The repeated reference to the war as a 'fateful struggle' came to mean that it was not a question of 'war' but merely of a struggle which had been forced on the nation against its will. The blame was put on forces which operated in secret and tried to deny Germany its right to living space. According to Nazi propaganda, Germany had always been surrounded by evil neighbours who had made war inevitable. In Louis Ralph's film *Heldentum und Todeskampf unserer Emden* (*The Heroic Fight to the Death of our Ship 'Emden'*, 1934), German sailors return from abroad after news of the outbreak of war in 1914 'to defend Germany against its innumerable enemies'.

Nazi terminology had several other euphemisms to conceal unpleasant facts. 'Special treatment' meant murder. The word 'voluntary' lost its meaning in a speech of Hitler's in 1935 to mark the inauguration of the Winter Charity tax: 'You *must* come forward and make *voluntary* sacrifices.' The reality behind the word 'euthanasia' was camouflaged by its translation into German as 'death on demand'.

The understatement of war in Third Reich language derives originally from soldiers' jargon during the First War — something which is particularly noticeable in Karl Ritter's films. Von Richthofen, the legendary flying hero of the First War who is frequently invoked in Third Reich air films, is reported to have said things like: 'After I've shot down an Englishman, my passion for hunting is satisfied for a quarter of an hour; which means that I can't shoot down two Englishmen in a row.' And: 'The weather has got really bad, so we can't assume that we'll have the luck of the hunt.' One might compare Saint-Exupéry: 'War is not real adventure, it is a substitute for adventure. An adventure is characterised by the wealth of relationships it produces, by the problems it poses, by the creative acts it occasions. One cannot turn a game like "heads or tails" into a real adventure by fixing the stakes at life or death. War is not an adventure, it is a disease. Like typhoid fever.'

The ideas underlying Third Reich war propaganda can be seen in the war newsreel compilation *Sieg im Westen* (*Victory in the West*, 1941), produced by the Army High Command. The illustrated programme booklet issued with the film states that it was designed to show the audacity of the German offensive and the superiority of German arms. The struggle is presented as a difficult one, since Germany's enemies are opposed to peace and the objective must be their annihilation. The film deals with three themes. We are shown first 'the dimension of the strategic planning and the daring of the operation' by means of animated maps designed to illustrate 'the leadership's brilliance'. The second aim is to demonstrate the superiority of German arms, with particular emphasis on tank battles. Thirdly, the film pays tribute to the

Plans for war: Goebbels with members of the military propaganda unit

unknown men of the assault battalions. In his contribution to the programme booklet, the head of the 'Army Press Section, Army Propaganda Unit, Army High Command' comments that the film 'shows in a very concise form the course of Germany's destiny' and reveals 'the values for which we are fighting today: Führer, People, Nation'.

The film has rightly been described as history 'seen from above'. It is not concerned with the grim everyday realities of war nor with the individual soldier's actions. The aim is to convince both the German population and allied, neutral and enemy countries of the superiority of German arms and Germany's overall war strategy. The enemy is shown to be brave; otherwise the victory would not be so impressive. It is regretted that the enemy commanders have forced their soldiers to put up a futile resistance against the German army. Germany's so-called 'encirclement' is illustrated with pictures of prisoners-of-war from exotic countries: to fight Germany, the enemy had to employ Negroes. Though the film, like the wartime newsreels, is designed to make the audience feel that they are eye-witnesses of the war, the reality of the fighting is never shown. The commentary describes the planning of military operations as if they were the preliminary moves in a game of chess;

condenses a long series of bloody encounters into fast, smooth-running movements on an animated map; and then immediately illustrates the result of the action with reports from the front. This technique also serves to heighten the impression of a blitzkrieg.

If one were to take *Victory in the West* and similar documentaries at face value, the war was a continuous and irresistible forward movement. That heavy fighting means human casualties and soldiers wounded in action and returning as invalids was something the audience was not supposed to know. War is a gigantic panorama, a battle painting by Adolf Hitler, in which the individual soldier is seen only as an anonymous part of the rank and file of the mighty army. In this respect the Third Reich war film is the opposite of the Soviet war film, which makes a point of presenting individual stories and showing the action 'from below'. The effect produced by the Nazi propaganda perspective is illustrated by an incident reported in the New York *Times* of 26 February 1942. A German pilot who had taken part in an air-raid on Leningrad expressed his astonishment, on being taken prisoner, that Leningrad was not an abstract target, a dot on the map, but was a city full of living people.

Newsreels, streamlined in 1940 under the heading 'German Newsreel', were supervised by Goebbels at every stage of their production. Their effect on the population was very carefully analysed in secret reports – known as 'Reports from the Reich' – compiled twice weekly on all sections of the population by trusted officials of the SS security service. At the beginning of the war, German newsreels generally ran for eight weeks and were about 300 metres (11 minutes) long. By doubling the number of copies during the war, newsreels circulated for half this time while their length was considerably increased. Previously a short introductory item, newsreels became, because of their topicality and length, a main attraction. In an analysis of the political function of the newsreel, Hans-Joachim Giese comments that in June 1940 'cinema attendances had risen by about 90% compared to the same month in the previous year – a fact attributable to the outstanding quality of the German war newsreel'. In 1942 the average newsreel was 900 metres (33 minutes) long. About 2,000 prints of each newsreel were made. Every week more than 30,000 metres of film came in from the front, and from the more important actions as much as 50,000 metres. In 1942, a thousand prints of each exported newsreel were made, distributed to 34 countries in 29 languages; in 1939, the figures had been 41 prints sent to 16 countries. During the first three years of the war, 2·8 million metres of film were shot on the various fronts, and weekly audiences numbered about 20 million.

The newsreels made clever use of music and editing for manipulative purposes. Goebbels and his subordinates employed sophisticated techniques when they incorporated the newsreel into their propaganda of lies. The sheer impact of what was on the screen meant that the audience was given no opportunity at all to ask questions about what was being systematically suppressed. At the time of the German defeats, newsreel reports of the fighting were so delayed that the public was kept unaware of just how close the enemy threat was. With the Allies already on German soil, newsreel maps were still showing foreign placenames.

Goebbels himself took the leading part in the newsreel for 27 February 1943, which he described in his diary as 'a really masterly visual representation of a mass rally'. On 18 February 1943, in front of a carefully selected audience which included hundreds of well-drilled cheerleaders, Goebbels made his call for total war. Speaking as though his audience represented the whole nation, he said that the German people had been purified by the defeat at Stalingrad. 'In front of our enemies, who are listening to us on their radios', Goebbels asked ten questions. Each of them was answered with a unanimous shout of 'Yes', and particularly the fourth question: 'Do you want total war? Do you want it, if it has to be, more total, more radical than we can possibly imagine today?' During the shouts of 'Heil!' following the fifth question – 'Is your confidence in the Führer greater, surer, more unshakeable than ever?' – flags were raised as 'the highest token of homage'. With the words 'Now, people, rise up – and storm, burst forth!', the speech ended. Ursula von Kardorff recorded in her *Notes* how a journalist who was at the Sportpalast as a reporter, a 'quiet, thoughtful man and an anti-Nazi', found himself 'jumping up with the rest and on the point of joining in the shouting when he fell back into his seat ashamed. He said that if Goebbels had gone on to ask "Do you all want to die?", they would have howled "Yes!" to this as well.' The 'Reports from the Reich' confirmed that 'this film report significantly increased the propaganda effectiveness of the Sportpalast rally and in addition had a marked influence even on those who up to now had remained sceptical. And when they saw it in pictures, even the more cautious elements of the population were unable to resist the visibly overwhelming effect of the speech and the conspicuous response of those present at the rally.'

According to Hippler, State Controller of film, total war was to revise the 'soldiers and weapons' concept of war. 'In a total war,' he wrote, 'nations fight each other as wholes, and every expression of a nation's being is a weapon in the war – no matter whether it weakens the enemy nation's fighting spirit or stimulates that of one's own country; that is to say, by offering diversion, concentration and relaxation.' This remark indirectly encompasses the various categories of German war film. The entertainment film was by no means undervalued. As Goebbels put it: 'To wage war we need a country which keeps its spirit up. Battles are not won by a dispirited people.'

Entertainment in the service of the people: *Die grosse Liebe*

At a wartime conference of the State Film Department on 15 February 1941, Goebbels emphasised the 'national morale-boosting' function of the cinema – 'its function as a means of enabling and training a nation to carry through its vital mission. This can sometimes be achieved by entertainment. Entertainment can occasionally have the purpose of supporting a nation in its struggle for existence, providing it with the edification, diversion and relaxation needed to see it through the drama of everyday life. But that is only its incidental purpose. By which I mean that today film has to serve a political function. It is a means of educating the people. This process of education – and whether it is open or concealed makes no difference – is a prerogative of the government.'

An analysis of the most successful German films between 1940 and 1942 reveals that entertainment films with an openly political function, comedies whose plots were quite unconnected with everyday reality, and directly political propaganda films ran each other close in popular favour. Rolf Hansen's *Die grosse Liebe* (*Great Love*, 1942), a melodrama designed to show how 'every war has a profound effect on human affairs', and Eduard von Borsody's *Wunschkonzert* (*Request Concert*, 1940), a cross-section of social

The true German woman: Luise Ullrich in *Annelie*

attitudes during the first phase of the war, head the list with box-office figures of 8 million and 7·6 million Marks respectively. Next come Georg Jacoby's *Frauen sind doch bessere Diplomaten* (*Women are Better Diplomats*, 1941), the first German colour feature, a musical comedy set in the Biedermeier period (state category: 'popularly distinguished'), and Willi Forst's *Wiener Blut* (*Vienna Blood*, 1942), a musical costume piece set at the time of the Congress of Vienna. Both films had box-office takings of 7 million Marks. After these come eleven films whose openly political motivation cannot have been in doubt. These are the two Veit Harlan films *Jud Süss* (1940; box-office figures, 6·2 million Marks) and *Der grosse König* (*The Great King*, 1942; 6 million Marks); Liebeneiner's *Ich klage an* (*I Accuse*, 1941; 5·3 million Marks) and *Die Entlassung* (*The Dismissal*, 1942; 6 million Marks); Hans Steinhoff's *Ohm Krüger* (1941; 5·5 million Marks); Gustav Ucicky's *Heimkehr* (*Homecoming*, 1941; 4·9 million Marks); Rabenalt's ... *reitet für Deutschland* (*Riding for Germany* ..., 1941; 5 million Marks); Willi Forst's *Operette* (1940; 5 million Marks); Kurt Hoffmann's *Quax, der Bruchpilot* (*Quax, the Crash Pilot*, 1941; 5 million Marks); and Josef von Baky's *Annelie* (1941) – the story of a frivolous girl who is always arriving late (even for her birth) but who is transformed into a heroic Second World War mother — which took 6·5 million Marks. Along with these great political hits came Carl Froelich's *Hochzeit auf Bärenhof* (*Wedding at Bärenhof*, 1942), with 6 million Marks.

In 1937, in *Urlaub auf Ehrenwort* (*Leave on Parole*, directed by Karl Ritter), Felix Lützkendorf, the scriptwriter of *Request Concert*, had interwoven episodes from different milieux in a story whose common denominator was the glorification of the wartime community spirit. Lützkendorf's work, which also included two other Karl Ritter films, *Über alles in der Welt* and *Stukas*, drew on every social class, as did the two Ritter films scripted by Fred Hildenbrand, *Pour le Mérite* and *Besatzung Dora* (*The Crew of the Dora*). Beauty, love and heroism in the classical sense are reserved for the higher classes of society, represented by dashing officers and elegant though strong and often intelligent girls. Ordinary people — bakers, butchers, tram conductors, artisans and their dependable wives — are shown in civilian life to be simple souls; and in war, as privates and NCOs, they know their place and respectfully obey their superior officers. It is not just that these Nazi films portray a social order in which jokes can never be made at the expense of the upper classes; their comedy always depends on crude popular stereotypes.

In *Request Concert*, it is some years before the leading characters, a girl called Inge and Flight Lieutenant Koch, who had first met during the 1936 Olympics, eventually find each other again. He is unable to write to her after he has been posted to Spain, and she is left believing that he has forgotten her. Three years later the war breaks out, and the men from Inge's town leave for the front. It is all one big, happy community — the teacher whose wife is expecting a child, the music student who plays Beethoven for the last time to the tenants of the house, and the small shopkeepers on the ground floor. The 'Request Concert'* ties a 'magic bond' between those at the front and those at home. Heinz Goedecke announces Captain Koch's request — the Olympic fanfare to remind him of the Olympics — and Inge knows that he is still thinking of her. A children's choir sings, and the teacher is told of the birth of his son. The musician has been killed in action, and the programme includes 'Good night, Mother' for his mother. Two soldiers bring in five pigs — 'booty captured from the enemy' — and report their mission completed. The Berlin Philharmonic plays Mozart, Marika Rökk sings a popular hit song, Weiss Ferdl tells jokes which are supposed to be risky, Heinz Rühmann, Hans Brausewetter and Josef Sieber liven up the atmosphere with the song 'You can't shock a sailor'. Something for everybody, in fact.

* A popular Sunday afternoon radio programme.

From prima donna to officer's wife: Zarah Leander in *Die grosse Liebe*, a box-office winner of 1942

Great Love resembles *Request Concert* in its account of the obstacles which lovers have to overcome and in its portrait of a community which by this time is feeling the threat of war on the home front. The film is about a celebrated Scandinavian singer who, through her love for an airforce officer, learns what it is to be a German soldier's wife. In the air-raid shelter she even takes an active part in the life of the local community. The spoiled prima donna discovers that people are not after all so 'awful', and in the end she even sings for the German troops in Paris. The lieutenant whose sense of duty is stronger than his love is contrasted with a composer, with the un-German name of Ruchnitzky, who when war comes continues to think only of his love for the singer, and is thus unworthy of her. When the film is shown today, the scenes in the air-raid shelter and at the concert which the singer gives for the soldiers in occupied France are usually omitted. The songs in the film became popular hit tunes with uplifting titles like 'I Know there'll be a Miracle' and 'The World's not Going to End Because of This'.

Oddly enough, the Army High Command did not recognise the film's propaganda qualities. Goebbels recorded in his diary on 23 May 1942 that Goering had complained to him about the Army High Command 'because it has protested about the new Leander film. This film is about an airforce officer who spends a night with a famous singer. The Army High Command considers itself morally insulted by this and insists that an airforce lieutenant would not do such a thing. Goering rightly objects to this on the grounds that an airforce lieutenant who didn't make use of an opportunity like this has no business being an airforce lieutenant. Goering makes fun of the High Command for being so prudish, which is absolutely fine with me since the High Command gives me a lot of trouble in my film work.'

On the other hand, *The Crew of the Dora*, which Karl Ritter made in 1942–43, was banned in November 1943 because of the worsening war situation. In this film the campaign on the Eastern Front is illustrated from the point of view of the average man, in this case one who comes home on leave and fires a simple girl with his dream of settling in the East after the war. It was hardly plausible for there to be talk about a farm in Russia in a propaganda film which would have been released at a time when not even the most credulous viewer could be persuaded that Hitler would conquer the Soviet Union.

In Helmut Käutner's *Goodbye, Franziska* (1941), it is the woman who reminds the man of his duty in time of war. He is a reporter who is always leaving his wife Franziska, drawn by the spectacle of war in strange continents. It is only the death of a friend in the Far East which makes him realise that his real place is the German town where Franziska and their children are waiting for him. Meanwhile war has broken out in Europe. Franziska wants her husband to go to the front; and when he refuses to leave her alone again so soon, she answers: 'But you managed to do it for thrills and adventure for all those years. And now, when there's some meaning to it at last, you can't do it?' The film ends with Michael and Franziska saying goodbye to each other at the station, as they have so often done before. But this time Franziska is one of many German soldiers' wives, and what she says is echoed by all the mothers, wives and daughters left behind on the platform: 'All I want is to love you and wait for you until at last, when there is peace again, you will stay with me for ever.'

There were a number of films directed specifically at young people. Victor de Kowa's *Kopf hoch, Johannes!* (*Chin up, Johannes!*, 1941) is the story of a spoiled South American landowner's son who is 'brought home again' when he enters a National Political school. Like the 'cadets' in Karl Ritter's film of that name, he is given the chance to prove that he is 'one of the boys'. Roger von Norman's *Himmelhunde* (*Hounds of the Sky*, 1942) and Alfred Weidenmann's *Junge Adler* (*Young Eagles*, 1944) are also aimed at the soldiers of tomorrow. In all these films the family is replaced by a community organised on military lines and deliberately designed to equip boys for war.

Love and duty: station farewell in *Auf Wiedersehen, Franziska* (Marianne Hoppe, Hans Söhnker)

Where the home upbringing fails, the 'spirit' which will win the war for National Socialism is triumphant. At the same time there is an attempt to dispel the lingering doubts which parents may have felt about the Party youth organisation. The 'cadets' wear uniforms from the Seven Years' War, but an introductory title informs us that 'German boys of today are of the same flesh and blood.' Facile clichés are the norm: 'Ah, a Frenchman – yes, they think fast.' Anyone losing his nerve on the firing line, or incapable of submitting to discipline, pays for it with his life.

In *Young Eagles* discipline and obedience are 'rules of the game', but flying is 'a kind of religion'. Intellectuals and violinists have a hard time of it, since 'anyone can make good music with a decent file in his hand'. The extent to which the country had come to depend on its young people in this penultimate year of the war can be gauged from the way the film emphasises the efforts of these 'young eagles', one of whom can now proudly claim: 'The factory is looking to us. Suddenly we're no longer nobodies.'

The pilots in *Stukas* are an equally closely-knit community. In one scene their commander, Captain Bork, and the squadron doctor, Gregorius, are playing 'Siegfried's Journey to the Rhine' as a piano duet. The music affects

A perspective on war: *Besatzung Dora*

the pilots 'like an echo of the battle they have just fought, and an overture to their next action when the squadron will be in the thick of the fire from 40 Hurricanes'. A flying officer, who has been shot down and is recovering in a field hospital well away from the front, is suffering from apathy, which in the opinion of his nurse can only be cured by a great experience. She suggests to the doctor that the invalid should be sent to Bayreuth: 'No one can come away from there without being deeply moved.' The *Illustrierter Filmkurier* reported the success of this therapy: 'The sound of the familiar Siegfried motif inspires memories of the day of the battle and the squadron's wonderful *esprit de corps*, memories so overwhelming that he suddenly feels liberated from his heavy, unreal burden and takes the quickest road back to Bork and his comrades.'

Similarly bizarre scenes are to be found in *Über alles in der Welt* (1941). Wiegand, the Paris correspondent of a Berlin newspaper, is arrested when war breaks out, and then courted by the League of Human Rights and the British Secret Service, who want to use his name for their anti-German propaganda. The League is represented by the Jewish Leo Samek, who is of course a mean-spirited coward. Wiegand pretends to accept the proposal so

The Nazi view of foreign agents: *Über alles in der Welt*

that he can escape and get back to Germany. One episode has him sitting in an open-air café during a German air-raid on Paris, enjoying the German bombing while everybody else takes refuge in the shelters. He manages to escape. Wounded and bleeding, he reaches the German lines. What matter that both his legs are shattered – he is in Germany again. Along with this individual story, the film includes scenes of Luftwaffe and Navy units in action. Also among the Germans who find themselves abroad when war breaks out are the members of an Austrian country band. The various plots are interwoven to suggest the universality of the war effort, to which no individual can contribute in more than a minor capacity. While all the Germans in the film are dogged fighters who really do put their country 'above all else in the world', the enemy is represented as insidious and treacherous in their propaganda tactics and in the way they fight. Today's audience would no longer find the anti-German remarks in the film grotesque; but for a Nazi film the idea that the 'Führer' could lose the war was both ludicrous and heretical. Accusing the enemy of tactics you use yourself is characteristic of the self-evident schizophrenia of Nazi propaganda.

This is very clearly demonstrated by *Heimkehr* (*Homecoming*), first shown in the autumn of 1941 and intended to remind the nation, at a critical stage in the Russian campaign, of the official purpose of the war: the foundation of an empire in which there would be room for every German and which had eliminated all opposition to Hitler's territorial ambitions. The reason for the war had already been explained in the prologue to Viktor Tourjanksy's film *Feinde* (*Enemies*, 1940): 'Humanity will never forget the untold suffering of the German people in Poland, for whom the whole of the postwar period was a time of unceasing victimisation. Deprived of their political rights, economically exploited, terrorised and dispossessed – this was their fate over the years. Then in 1939 the British guarantee to Poland precipitated the Polish massacres. Tens of thousands of innocent Germans were deported under threat of horrible torture. 60,000 were slaughtered like cattle.'

Gustav Ucicky's 'Film of the Nation' * about the 'homecoming' of a group of German-speaking people shows the Poles as brutal oppressors of a peaceful minority which had preserved its German identity in a hostile environment and which would have been exterminated if Hitler had not come to the rescue of his tormented fellow-countrymen. There is no indication of the pressure exerted by Hitler on Poland, which had occasioned the British guarantee to preserve the independence of Poland after Hitler's entry into Prague had shown that it was not only the repatriation of Germans abroad which interested him but the domination of Europe, and not only of Europe. *Homecoming* reveals the hallmarks of Nazi terror tactics – but calls them *Polish* provocation and *Polish* brutality. It only needs a change of uniform at the military parade (a provocative demonstration of strength), and a different national anthem from the one which a small minority refuses to sing (for which they are set on by a frenzied mob), and the schizophrenic character of this propaganda is plain. The outbreak of war is preceded in the film by a number of scenes in which decent Germans are attacked by cowardly, subhuman Poles whose crimes include stoning a girl to death after triumphantly wrenching a swastika medallion from her neck. The Polish Foreign Minister's apology for such incidents to Germany's diplomatic representative is cynical and hypocritical. But the really curious scenes are those in which a group of Germans, drawing comfort from a Hitler speech which they are secretly listening to on the radio, are arrested and thrown into the cellar of a dark prison, where they wait to be shot at dawn. Before German planes arrive to send the Poles running and German tanks mow down the prison walls, the captive Germans discuss their plight. The blind visionary, who in the final scene says of his homeland, now reclaimed, 'I can see it there, stretching far, far, far away into the distance,' is talking to his daughter in the prison:

* A designation, rarely bestowed, to films considered to make an outstanding contribution to the national cause.

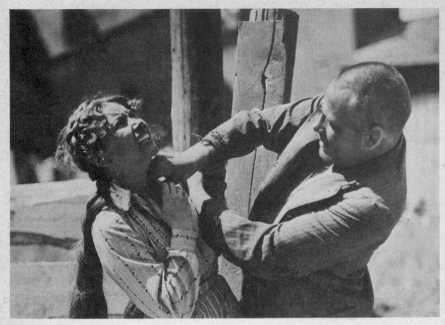

Heimkehr: German innocent and 'subhuman' Pole

FATHER: People locked in cellars and shot. Through the window with a machine-gun. And you lie in your bed and don't know anything about it. Or don't want to know. Because if you did know, you couldn't sleep a wink. You're thinking, my God, that salami I had this evening didn't agree with me, I've got a belly-ache. You get up and go into the kitchen and take a spoonful of sodium bicarbonate. And that's the end of that. Death's all around you, and nobody gives a damn about all the misery and suffering and fear and despair that's spreading – it doesn't mean a thing to you. Where's the heart that gets indignant about this? Where's the mouth that calls out that everything is upside-down in the world, as upside-down as the people who live next to each other without living together? Where's the mind that starts thinking about how we can make it different? Where's the voice that wakes up the whole world from its sleep of death? Where? Where?

DAUGHTER: In Germany!

FATHER: Yes, that's it, in Germany. You're right, my girl, the voice is heard all over the world now. It's startling people now, and it's only tragic that it has to speak with guns and dive-bombers. But there's no other way. Because otherwise nobody would listen to the message that we must put a stop to this goddamned selfishness. That you can't be allowed, you just can't be allowed to lie in your bed while someone else is freezing to death on the street. You can't be allowed to pat your stomach and have a satisfied burp – 'My God, I'm full!' – while every hour, every minute, every second even, hundreds of thousands of human beings are moaning in the last agonies of starvation, if they can still moan at all. And now we're standing here in this damp cellar waiting. You know what we're waiting for – yes, you know what it is. Perhaps we still have an hour's grace, or half an hour, or a quarter of an hour . . .

DAUGHTER: Even if we don't live to see it, Father, at least we know, don't we, that there will be others after us who will live to see it, and that's a kind of comfort; and also that we who have lived together can also die together and not each of us on his own in despair.

The climax of this prison scene is the speech the daughter makes to rouse the spirits of her fellow-prisoners:

Friends, we're going to get home, that's for sure. It's quite certain, somehow we'll get home. And why shouldn't we? Everything is possible, and this isn't just possible, it's certain. At home in Germany people are no longer weak, and they're no longer unconcerned at what happens to us. On the contrary – as Fritz is always telling me – they're very interested in us. And why shouldn't we be able to go home if that's what we want? Think how it will be, friends, think how it will be when everything around us is German, and when you go into a shop it won't be Yiddish or Polish you hear but German! And it won't only be the whole village that will be German, everything all round us will be German. And we'll be right in the middle of it, in the heart of Germany. Think how it will be, friends! And why shouldn't it be so? We'll be living

'German like us': the prison scene in *Heimkehr* (Paula Wessely)

71

on the good old warm soil of Germany. In our own country and at home. And at night, in our beds, when we wake from sleep, our hearts will suddenly beat quicker with the sweet knowledge that we are sleeping in Germany, at home in our own country, and all around us is the comforting night and a million German hearts beating softly and as one — you are at home, my friend, at home with your own people. It will be a really marvellous feeling for us, that the seeds in the fields and the crops and the rocks and the waving grass and the swaying branches of the hazelnut bushes and the trees — that all this is German. German like us, and belonging to us, because it has all grown from the millions of German hearts which have been laid to rest in the earth and have turned into German soil. Because we don't only live a German life, we also die a German death. And even when we are dead we are still German, a real part of Germany. A handful of soil for our grandchildren to grow corn in. And from our hearts the vines will grow high in the sun — the sun which doesn't burn them but shines brightly on them and gives the grapes their sweetness. And all around the birds are singing and everything is German.

This is what the war was all about. Everything must be German. What was called 'home' already included the old German Reich, Austria and Czechoslovakia; then came Poland, and soon all good Germans living there were to be spared the prospect of hearing 'Yiddish or Polish' spoken. Hitler had written in *Mein Kampf*: 'When today we speak of new soil, new ground in Europe, we may think in the first instance of Russia and her neighbouring dependent states.'

And tomorrow the whole world.

6. No Right to Live

In the thousand-year Reich of National Socialism, the Jews had no right to live. In his 'men's hostel' in Vienna's Meldemannstrasse, the young, unemployed, half-starved odd-man-out Adolf Hitler had already formed an image of the Jews as the embodiment of evil. History was to him a life and death struggle between light and dark, in which ultimately the dark-haired inferior races would be exterminated by the fair-skinned Teutons. It was necessary for him to believe in the differences between men and races in order to count himself among the superior beings. According to Hitler's definition, the difference between Germans and Jews was not only the difference between supermen and apemen, but also the antithesis between the law of the strong — which he was constantly preaching — and the teachings of the Bible. Hitler predicted that 'the day will come when I shall replace the Ten Commandments with the tablets of a new law, and history will honour our movement as a great struggle for the liberation of mankind from the curse of Sinai. For this is what we are fighting, the curse of the so-called morality which decrees that the weak should be protected from the strong. We are defending the eternal law of battle, the great law of Nature, against the so-called Ten Commandments.'

The Jews were not the only community whose existence was threatened from the very beginning of the Third Reich. As early as 14 July 1933 a law had been passed 'to prevent the spread of hereditary diseases', providing the basis for the euthanasia programme and the experiments on concentration camp prisoners. Hitler justified the extermination of persons considered 'unfit to live', racially 'inferior' or debilitated by illness with this policy declaration in *Mein Kampf*: 'A stronger generation will displace the weak, since the life force in its final form will always break the ludicrous chains of the so-called humanitarianism of the individual, and replace it with a humanitarianism of Nature which will destroy the weak to make room for the strong.'

Hitler needed the Jews as a permanent scapegoat on which the mass movement under his control could work off their resentment. In conversation with Rauschning,* Hitler said that the Jew 'should not be over-estimated as an enemy'. If he did not exist he would have to be invented, since it was necessary to have 'a visible enemy and not just an invisible one'. The genius of a great leader, according to *Mein Kampf*, consists in knowing how to concentrate the hate of his followers on one single enemy so that 'if need be even traditional opponents will unite against this enemy'. In his study *The Fanatic*, Eric Hoffer shows how Hitler used the Jews as a kind of model devil, omnipotent and omnipresent, and in his propaganda populated the entire world outside Germany with Jews or Jewish henchmen who were unceasingly working against him and so against Germany. Hoffer describes how Hitler used resentment of the Jews not merely to build a united front in Germany against the movement towards 'world peace', but also 'to undermine the will to resist in the anti-semitic countries of Poland, Rumania, Hungary and finally even France. He made similar use of anti-Communism.'

Jewish resistance in Germany was paralysed by the fact that the persecution was stepped up slowly and in stages, so that Hitler's real objective – mass murder – was only clearly apparent when the Jews were completely weakened and demoralised. At first, despite persistent threats and unprecedented legislative measures, the majority of both persecuted and persecutors were unwilling to believe that Hitler was seriously determined to put his *Mein Kampf* programme into operation. Phrases like 'A civilised nation does not behave like that' or 'This can't happen to decent people' lulled the Jews into a false sense of security, a security which the Third Reich was not going to give them. As good Germans they could not understand that the authorities had criminal intentions, and were ready to put them into practice. The anti-semitic measures meant restrictions for the Jews, but they were legally enacted and for centuries Jewish history had known laws operating against the Jews.

The boycott of Jewish shops on 1 April 1933, as well as the so-called

* Leader of the Danzig Nationalists.

Crystal Night (10 November 1938) when hundreds of synagogues were burned down, thousands of Jewish shops looted, and 20,000 Jews deported to concentration camps, were dress rehearsals for the 'final solution of the Jewish question'. On 30 January 1939 Hitler made his first direct reference to the extermination of the Jews. In a speech to the Reichstag he said: 'If international Jewish finance, both in Europe and outside, should succeed in plunging nations into another world war, the result would not be a victory for Jewry but the eradication of the Jewish race in Europe.' During the war which even then he was planning but for which he officially denied responsibility, blaming it on the Jews, Hitler referred again to this speech: 'You will remember the Reichstag meeting at which I said, "If the Jews imagine they can start a world war in order to exterminate the European races, the result will not be the extermination of the European races but the extermination of European Jewry." You have always laughed at my prophecies. A large number of those who laughed then are no longer laughing today. Those who are still laughing will probably also stop laughing before very long.'

In October 1939 Hitler signed a decree legalising euthanasia, backdating it to 1 September, the day war broke out. The deportation of Jews from Austria and Czechoslovakia to Poland began on 12 October 1939; on 23 November the wearing of the Yellow Star was made compulsory in the General Government area; and by 10 February 1940 Jews were being deported from Germany to the East. The inflammatory anti-semitic films produced by the Third Reich were intended to justify these actions; more than that, they had to contribute towards turning decent citizens into compliant mass murderers. Significantly, the most important anti-Jewish propaganda films were made in 1939 and 1940.

The first two films, Hans H. Zerlett's *Robert and Bertram* and Heinz Helbig's *Leinen aus Irland* (*Linen from Ireland*), incorporate their caricature of the subhuman Jew within the framework of a comedy. Both films illustrate a recurring theme of Nazi propaganda: that the Jew is crafty but not clever. Nordic cunning defeats Jewish guile. 1940 saw three films concerned with the 'Jewish danger' in which Jews are no longer comic figures but subhumans. These films were Erich Waschneck's *The Rothschilds*, Veit Harlan's *Jud Süss* and Fritz Hippler's 'documentary' *Der ewige Jude* (*The Wandering Jew*). Also made in the same year was Wolfgang Liebeneiner's *Bismarck*, which was originally to have been about the English Jews' campaign against the founder of the Second Reich. I have seen the text of a number of anti-semitic scenes which were to feature in the film but were never shot. Only one episode survives, an abortive attempt by a Jew to assassinate Bismarck. Jews appear as foils for the heroes of two 1941 films, Ritter's *Über alles in der Welt* and Herbert Selpin's *Carl Peters*, but they are now marginal characters, as they are in Ucicky's *Homecoming*, Rabenalt's *Riding for Germany* . . . and Hans H. Zerlett's *Venus on Trial*, all made in 1941. They already belong to yesterday's world. Thanks to the policies of the Führer, they are no longer a threat.

According to the records of the so-called Conference of Ministers at the Reich Propaganda Ministry (published in Willi A. Boelcke's book *Kriegspropaganda 1939–1941*), Goebbels considered these three films – *Jud Süss*, *The Rothschilds* and *The Wandering Jew* – so important that he issued special instructions to the press. On 26 April 1940 he announced that the press 'publicity campaign for the films *Jud Süss* and *Die Rothschilds* should not refer to them as anti-semitic films'. Audiences were to believe that these films showed 'Jewry as it really is'. 'If they seem anti-semitic, this is not because they are aiming for any particular bias.'

The *Völkischer Beobachter* review of *Jud Süss*, quoted later in this chapter, reveals just how closely this instruction was followed. Behind the Propaganda Minister's order lurks his conviction that propaganda only achieves its desired objective when it is taken not for propaganda but for the truth. In a speech to the film industry on 15 February 1941, Goebbels stated that it was necessary to act on the principle that 'the intention should not be revealed to avoid irritating people'.

In *Robert and Bertram* the commercial councillor Ipelmeyer, a *nouveau riche* Jew, is duped by the two crafty heroes, characters drawn from traditional comedy. The film's Jewish characters are grossly caricatured, uneducated blockheads who are naturally incapable of concealing their origins in the narrow streets of the ghetto. The point being made by the film is that the Jew must pay the price: the 'swindler' is himself swindled. It is apparently permissible to rob a Jew, since according to anti-semitic propaganda a Jew only acquires his property through swindling and theft. When a guest at the masked ball in Ipelmeyer's house admiringly exclaims that Ipelmeyer's palace must have cost a fortune, the answer is that 'it cost more than that, but not to Herr Ipelmeyer, to the people he has swindled'.

In *Linen from Ireland* the ambitious Dr Kuhn (once called Kohn, of course) tries, in his capacity of Secretary of a large textile firm in Prague, to extend his domination of the Central and Eastern European textile market 'so as to acquire a decisive influence on the world market'. He hopes that this will help him conquer Lilly, daughter of the firm's President, who trusts him blindly. Kuhn applies to the Ministry of Trade for permission to import duty-free linen from Ireland, which would give the firm a tremendous boost and at the same time ruin the Sudetenland weavers. The racially conscious blonde naturally rejects his advances, and Kuhn's scheme is thwarted by an incor-

Jewish caricature in *Leinen aus Irland*

ruptible Ministry official who then carries off the beautiful Lilly. In this film the Jew is only dangerous because the indolent bureaucrats in Vienna fail to see what he is up to. The *Illustrierter Filmkurier* also made the point that the action is set during the time of the Habsburg monarchy, which is 'already showing clear signs of decadence, and national and social problems in urgent need of solution.' A fact which is incidentally used to justify the need for the *Anschluss* of Austria within the Reich. In a state governed by National Socialists a domestic craft like weaving is protected against the international machinations of dark forces such as those represented by a Dr Kuhn. An elegant intriguer, Kuhn has repeatedly to be reminded of his origins by his uncle Sigi. Kuhn and Sigi are a lesson to the audience that the outward elegance of a Jew is only a façade behind which the alert anti-semite can immediately detect a craven and brutal cunning.

The caricatures of Jews in these films are reminiscent of the repugnant pictures of Jews in children's books through which the Third Reich was already drumming into the young a hatred of Jews. If you believe that Jews are not human beings but devils and vermin, you will be ready to obey when the order comes to exterminate them. By 1935 the Nuremberg Laws had

'A Jewish–British plutocracy': *Die Rothschilds*

already classified Jews as inferior, while half-Jews were identified as a dangerous blend of German and Jewish characteristics; and during the war the so-called 'first-grade half-breeds' were given the choice of sterilisation or deportation. For Jews of 'pure race' this alternative was not offered. As early as 21 September 1939, in a message to the heads of the Security Police task forces, Reinhard Heydrich referred to the 'final solution' of the Jewish question. Films like *The Wandering Jew*, *Jud Süss* and *The Rothschilds* provided justification for the Third Reich's Jewish policy, and prepared the population for measures whose precise schedules were in the first phase of the war still to be determined.

The Rothschilds combines anti-semitic and anti-British propaganda; though for Goebbels the British were 'the Jews among the Aryans', and by 1940 the British are characterised as tools of a Jewish world conspiracy. This film about the rise of the House of Rothschild includes lines like 'You say Rothschild, I mean England', and ends with this announcement: 'As this film was being completed, the last descendants of the Rothschilds fled Europe as refugees. The fight against their accomplices, the British plutocracy, continues.'

Die Rothschilds: 'the real victor of Waterloo' (Carl Kuhlmann)

The *Illustrierter Filmkurier* commented that *The Rothschilds* did not cover 'the whole Jewish problem' but only 'a prominent episode in the Jewish struggle for power in the milieu of capitalist England'. Before the audience has grasped that the Jewish and English plutocrats are 'worthy of each other', they are shown how the head of the House of Rothschild, with the help of £600,000 from the treasury of Count von Hessen, builds the foundations of the family empire, thus setting in motion the 'Jewifying' of England and the domination of the world by a 'Jewish–British plutocracy'. Old Rothschild expresses his admiration for the Count, who only takes $1\frac{1}{8}$% interest on his loan, for being a great trader in men – 'To make a lot of money, we have to take a lot of blood.' Since Jewish religious law, as is common knowledge, expressly forbids the consumption of blood, and in its commandment 'Thou shalt not kill' puts respect for every form of life at the centre of its beliefs, every Jewish character in Nazi films is therefore seen to be breaking the laws of his religious faith. In *The Rothschilds* we are shown international Jewry profiting from the war 'while nations are bleeding on the battlefields'. England's victory over Napoleon is 'a victory won by gold, a Rothschild victory, a victory for the Star of David'. The real victor of Waterloo is Nathan Rothschild, who spreads the news that Napoleon has won the battle and makes millions by buying up cheaply the shares sold off in panic on the stock exchange.

The kind of reception the film got in the summer of 1940 can be gauged from the newspaper comment. The *Deutsche Allgemeine Zeitung* saw 'devilish fumes rising from the witches' cauldron of the Jewish quest for gold, which bubbles over with swindling, trickery, cunning, revenge, smuggling and bribery'. Audiences could witness how 'this poison gnaws and eats away at the foundations of British capital, until the old classes, their property undermined, crumble away as the Ghetto triumphs over the City and Jerusalem usurps the power of the Empire'. *Der Film* found Nathan Rothschild wearing 'the features of Ahasverus – this has always been the Jew, this is the face he has worn for centuries, and there is no perceptible difference between the crooks of the Eastern ghettos, the big-time immigrant swindlers and the international financial racketeers'.

Jud Süss also creates the impression of a faithful re-enactment of a historical event. The illustrated brochure issued by the Terra-Filmkunst information service sets the tone: 'Clean-shaven and dressed like a gentleman, the Jew Süss Oppenheimer contrives to be appointed Finance Minister to the Duke of Württemberg ... Matching one another in treachery, the court Jew and Minister Süss Oppenheimer and his secretary outbid one another in tricks and intrigues to bleed the people of Württemberg ... The Jew Süss Oppenheimer violates the beautiful Dorothea Sturm, an outrageous act which confirms the extent of his guilt ... Jew, hands off German women!'

The historical Joseph Süss-Oppenheimer was born in Heidelberg in 1692, not in fact as the son of the Jewish director of a troupe of strolling players, but as the child of a liaison between the Freiherr von Heydersdorff and the daughter of a Jewish cantor in Frankfurt am Main. During the trial which ended with the death sentence being passed on the Jew Süss, he was described as the Freiherr's natural son, which in the terminology of the Third Reich's racial laws made him a half-caste and not a pure Jew. He was the Palatinate's Lord High Steward and war adviser when in 1732 he became acquainted with Prince Karl Alexander of Württemberg, who as a field commander was compared to Alexander the Great by his contemporaries and who in October 1733 became Duke of Württemberg. Süss-Oppenheimer was made his financial adviser, with the task of procuring the money to pay off the national debt. He took a lease on the Mint and made a huge profit, though the money he minted was at the time considered to be the best in the German Empire. The Württemberg Diet resisted the new financial measures and turned to the Duke, who, old soldier as he was, would brook no opposition and through the instigation of the Jesuits was turned against the Diet. The Duke's conflict with the Diet, in which Süss-Oppenheimer did not intervene, centred on his proposal to impose a military régime in a Protestant country, which would have invalidated the constitution and forced the people to turn Catholic. A coup was planned, but on the day it was to take place the Duke threw a fit of rage over the demands put forward by two deputations from the Diet, suffered a stroke and died.

Süss-Oppenheimer was arrested, and after a lengthy trial was condemned to death by hanging. The country's most celebrated lawyer, Harrprecht the Elder, said that in his opinion 'on the basis of the existing laws of the German Empire and the province of Württemberg the accused cannot be sentenced to death, but those of his goods which can be proved to have been acquired by fraud should be confiscated and he should be exiled from the dukedom.' Nevertheless, the death sentence was passed. The Ducal Administrator signed it in January 1738, remarking, 'It is a rare event that a Jew has to pay the price for Christian villainy.' The court, in confirming the sentence, omitted the only fact which would have justified the death penalty according to the laws of the time: the accused had enjoyed intimate relations with ladies of society, for which both he as a Jew and his Christian partners had risked the death penalty. But nobody was going to put members of respected Württemberg families on trial.

Jud Süss was the subject of a short story by Wilhelm Hauff (1827). Lion Feuchtwanger's novel *Jud Süss* – in which the Jews are portrayed as the

(above and opposite) *Jud Süss*: the prototype of the criminal Jew and the final solution (Werner Krauss, Ferdinand Marian)

eternal scapegoat — was published in 1925; and after the Nazi seizure of power served as the basis for a British film which had a pro-Jewish bias.

Veit Harlan's film, in contrast, makes Süss-Oppenheimer the prototype of the criminal Jew. Unlike his real historical counterpart, Süss here first meets the Duke after his accession, and uses his financial influence over the Duke to have the gates of Stuttgart opened to the Jews. In the film it is Süss who persuades the Duke to seize absolute power by staging a coup d'état. Also in the film Süss wants to marry the daughter of District Councillor Sturm; and when her father marries her instead to the notary Faber, Süss has him arrested on a trumped-up charge of plotting against the Duke. The fair-haired Dorothea's husband also falls into the Jew's hands, escaping torture only because Dorothea runs to Süss in despair. 'Süss sets Faber free. But at what price? A few hours after his release Faber fishes his young wife's body out of the river Neckar.' The most repugnant scenes in the film — apart from the sequence in which Faber's torture is cut short by a signal from a white handkerchief indicating that Dorothea has been raped — are the entry of the Jews into Stuttgart and the Jewish religious service, during which Süss appeals to his fellow-believers for financial support for the Duke. In the film

the death sentence is based on 'racial defilement', and Luther is invoked as an anti-semitic authority. That the film saw Württemberg in 1738 as a mirror of Europe in 1940, where there was no place for Jews, is clear from the final scene, a proclamation banning Jews from Württemberg. All Jews were to leave the area within a month. A spokesman for the Diet hopes that 'our descendants will keep an iron hand on this law, so that they may be spared harm to their lives and property and to the blood of their children and their children's children.'

The *Völkischer Beobachter* saw the Jud Süss story as a historical example 'which provides an awesome picture of the general situation'. The film was praised for its 'complete avoidance of bias, and its clear demonstration of how a previous attempt in miniature to subjugate a country foreshadowed the later aspirations towards domination of the whole globe.' The historical framework was intended to lend credibility to the caricatures of Jewish types. The notion that behind all his masks the Jew was always the same was underlined by having one actor – whose true 'German blood' had to be expressly authenticated – play several Jewish parts in the film, thereby illustrating, with demonic force, the theory that Jews are subhuman. The film was repeatedly shown to SS units before they were sent into action against Jews. It was shown to the non-Jewish population when the Jews were about to be deported.

Der Reichsführer-♯ Berlin, den 30. 9. 1940
Tgb. Nr. 35/142/40

Eing.: 76.10.40
Rg. :
Erl. :

Verteiler V

Ich ersuche Vorsorge zu treffen,
daß die gesamte ♯ und Polizei im Laufe des Winters
den Film "Jud Süß" zu sehen bekommt.

Der Reichsführer-♯:

Recommended viewing: Himmler's order that the SS and the police were to see *Jud Süss*

Concentration camp guards saw it. And at the Auschwitz trial in Frankfurt former SS Rottenführer Stefan Baretzki admitted that the effect of showing the film was to instigate maltreatment of prisoners.

There were several versions of the 'documentary film' produced by the Reich Propaganda Department of the National Socialist Party under the title *The Wandering Jew**. 'Sensitive souls' were advised to see the shorter version, from which the Jewish ritual slaughter sequences were omitted. The commentary by Eberhard Taubert was dropped in the foreign language versions of the film; its demagogic tone, aimed at German audiences, might have damaged the credibility of the 'document'. The effect of this was to give more prominence to the music, which here, as in other anti-Jewish propaganda films, took on a turgid Oriental flavour the moment Jews appeared on the screen. Shots of Nordic people, on the other hand, were accompanied by Bach. The film was mostly shot in the Jewish areas of Poland, though the commentary omits to mention that it was the Nazis themselves who were responsible for the dingy, cramped conditions of these ghettos. The opening sentence immediately sets the tone: 'The civilised Jews such as those we know in Germany provide an incomplete picture of their racial characteristics. This film shows original material shot in the Polish ghettos, shows us the Jews as they really looked before they concealed themselves behind the mask of civilised Europeans.'

The ghetto was 'a breeding ground of epidemics . . . endangering the health of the Aryan people'. The implication is that here was a menace which must be 'resisted'. A montage sequence of rats, calculated to leave an indelible impression on the minds of any audience, is accompanied by a commentary informing us that rats 'have followed men like parasites from the very beginning', destroying the country and spreading disease. 'They are cunning, cowardly and fierce, and usually appear in large packs. In the animal world they represent the element of insidious subterranean destruction.' 'Not dissimilar from the place Jews have among men,' the commentary continues, as the rats are followed by shots of Jews crowded together in the ghetto. It could hardly be stated more clearly: the killing of one or of many Jews was not a crime but a necessity. Jews, the film implies, are not human beings but pests which have to be exterminated.

This montage was duly applauded by the critics. The correspondent from the *Deutsche Allgemeine Zeitung* 'heaved a sigh of relief when the film ended with pictures of Germans and things German'. Apart from *The Wandering Jew*, distorted documentary material included several short exercises which in similar vein compared Jews with cockroaches. In my own films *Mein Kampf* and *Eichmann and the Third Reich*, I used material shot in the Warsaw ghetto

* Also known inappropriately in the context, as *The Eternal Jew*.

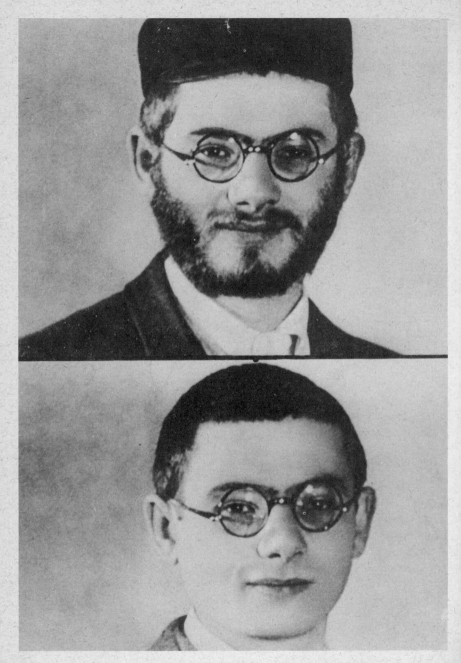

Always a Jew: 'documentary' evidence of assimilation in *Der ewige Jude*

but never shown publicly during the Third Reich. Emmanuel Ringelblum, the historian of the Warsaw ghetto, has described how the German film cameramen went about their work in the summer of 1942. Jews were herded together and then the Jewish security police were ordered to disperse them. Scenes showing very Jewish-looking men locked together in the ritual baths with young women were manufactured to create the impression that the Jews bathed together in the nude. A restaurant owner was forced to lay his tables to suggest to the audience an abundance of delicacies and champagne; then Jews were indiscriminately rounded up on the streets and filmed eating and drinking. Grocery shop windows were filled with rare delicacies before being filmed. These shots were supposed to convey to German audiences that the Jews in the ghettos were far too prosperous. The banquet was meant to incite envy and resentment among those who could not afford such expensive food. At the same time film of the miserable conditions in the ghetto was juxtaposed with doctored images of a fictitious prosperity; some of this material was used in a series of articles in the *Berliner Illustrierter* entitled 'Jews at home'. Jews were said to be cruel to each other, while the rich Jews of the ghetto were indifferent to the poor; and scenes were shot to prove this cruelty. A member of the Jewish security police is about to strike a Jew when a German runs up to stop him. A boy is made to steal a loaf of bread and run off with it to his friends, who are supposed to be hiding him and his loot. In reality there was hardly any bread in the ghetto, and the guards at the walls stopped any food being taken in. But in the film the little thief is protected from the baker and the police by a German. Beating children is wrong.

According to the commentary of *The Wandering Jew*, the ghetto's poor were not poor at all, but 'through decades of trading had hoarded enough money to make clean and comfortable homes for themselves and their families. Yet they continue to live for generations in the same dirty, flea-ridden holes.' In reality, according to Governor General Frank, the one consolation the Poles themselves had was that 'the Jews are even worse off'. While one of Himmler's aides was proposing that the Poles should be forced to practise birth control and should be allowed only four years of primary school education, the ghettos which the SS set up all over the East were being designated as the first phase in the physical annihilation of all Jews. They were deliberately located near railway lines; it would thus be no trouble to deport those who hadn't died on the spot to one of the extermination camps.

Nazi cameramen recorded every stage in the demoralisation process, filming starving people begging on the streets or lying outside their houses too weak to move; children who grew up in the shadow of death, plagued by vermin and disease, unsmiling and with no toys to play with, their eyes already old and accustomed to misery and death; epidemics raging in the ghetto – though there was of course no mention of the fact that these very epidemics were spread by the Nazis under the pretence of fighting them. There is also no reference in these filmed records to the fact that immediately after the defeat of Poland an area of ten square kilometres in Warsaw was transformed into a ghetto. This district had previously housed a population of 240,000 Jews and 80,000 non-Jews. Now the non-Jews had to move out to make room for hundreds of thousands of Jews forcibly transported to the ghetto. There were initially six people to every room in the ghetto, but this soon rose to thirteen to a room. People who only a few weeks before had been living a normal life found themselves forced to live and die like rats in the ghetto. Herein lies the cynicism of a 'document' like *The Wandering Jew*: people confined in a world of dirt like animals in overcrowded cages, and their subsequent degradation presented as though it were completely normal, an existence which these victims of the Nazi terror had supposedly chosen for themselves, a simple demonstration of the theory that Jews are not people like you and me.

The most harrowing sequerces from these Nazi films on the hell devised in the Polish ghettos for the victims of the 'final solution' were never used. It was by no means certain that the material would actually induce loathing and resentment in the general public. Preview audiences had in fact been sympathetic. And it was precisely the most vicious of the doctored sequences which produced this unintended effect. Pairs of Jewish men and women had been put in front of the camera to demonstrate social differences which had been contrived for these very shots, but the eyes of those filmed expressed something altogether different from what the cameramen had been trying to register. What was communicated was the silent despair of these humiliated people, who knew that what awaited them after the filming was an unknown and degrading death.

In 1945 representatives of the International Red Cross visited the Jewish 'model camp' at Theresienstadt (Terezin) in Czechoslovakia and were shown part of a film made there in the summer of 1944. Kurt Gerron, a once prominent actor who had emigrated to Holland in 1933, had fallen into the hands of the Gestapo there and was now a prisoner at the camp, was given the responsibility for writing and directing a film called *The Führer Gives the Jews a Town*, which was designed to reveal Theresienstadt as a 'paradise for Jews'. Like all other investigators, when I questioned survivors of Theresienstadt, I found some dispute about Gerron's contribution to the film and his motives for collaborating on it. When the film was completed, Gerron and most of the other leading collaborators were deported to Poland and gassed. At the very moment when the transports to the extermination camps were being got under way, thousands of Theresienstadt inmates were recruited as extras in a film designed to camouflage what was really happening in the camp. The film included a number of scenes with children, designed to create the impression that Theresienstadt was a particularly pleasant place for children to be. Since in the autumn of 1944 an estimated 1,600 children were deported from Theresienstadt, and in the Auschwitz selection process no child who looked under fourteen escaped the gas chamber, most of the children in the film must have been murdered soon after it was completed. There were shops in the film which were specially constructed for the cameras and in which there was nothing to buy. A stage was built for an open-air cabaret show at a spot which was normally out of bounds to prisoners. In the film's Theresienstadt, people are happily playing football, well-fed men stand under showers, coquettish girls are busy putting on make-up. In his book *The Hidden Truth*, H. G. Adler quotes as an example of the way in which the Nazis were planning to use film – but which to a large extent was by this time no longer feasible – a newsreel from the autumn of 1944 which juxtaposes a coffee-house scene shot in Theresienstadt with a montage of scenes from the front lines. The commentator remarks: 'While Jews in Theresienstadt sit enjoying coffee and cakes and dance around, our soldiers are bearing the brunt of this terrible war, the suffering and the hardship, to defend their homeland.'

In other respects the Jew in Nazi propaganda was a projection of his persecutors. The sexual excesses constantly reported in the *Stürmer* as typically Jewish in fact belonged to the experience and imagination of the *Stürmer's* editor, 'Frankenführer' Julius Streicher. When Hitler said of the Jews in *Mein Kampf*, 'Within the space of a few years he will seek to exterminate the nation's intelligentsia and reduce countries to a state of permanent enslavement by robbing them of their spiritual leaders,' he was providing an exact description of his own methods. The Nazis themselves developed the characteristics which they ascribed to the Jews. The propaganda fantasy of a Jewish world conspiracy found its reality in the Nazi Fifth Columns. The death of the Jew Süss in Veit Harlan's film is uncannily prophetic. His last words – 'I was only an obedient servant of my master' – anticipate the position adopted by innumerable Nazi criminals, big and small, in the postwar trials.

In accordance with Hitler's doctrine about the rights of the strong, the first people to be systematically exterminated were not the Jews but unhealthy Aryans. A film on the subject of hereditary diseases, *Opfer der Vergangenheit* (*Victim of the Past*, directed by Gernot Bock-Stieber), was shown in every one of Germany's 5,300 cinemas in 1937. The première at the Ufa-Pavillon in Berlin's Nollendorfplatz was graced by a speech from the co-founder and head of the National Socialist Medical Association, Dr Gerhard Wagner, who had commissioned this and similar efforts. Wagner had already raised the problem of euthanasia at the 1935 Nuremberg Party Rally, when the anti-Jewish Nuremberg Laws were also announced. The commentary of *Victim of the Past* refers to the prevention of the spread of hereditary diseases as a moral law: 'In practice it means charity and the highest respect for the God-given laws of nature. To prevent the growth of weeds is to promote the plants of value.' The film suggests that 'this law of natural selection has been frighteningly transgressed'. It was to misapply both Christianity and the laws of nature to nurse mentally 'inferior' criminals in an institution paid for by money 'which we could probably put to better use helping a good many strong, healthy, talented children in our population in their lives and careers.' This 'waste of German national wealth' was matched by 'a waste of soul and spirit, because we have tried to persuade ourselves that in making sacrifices for the most wretched and helpless of lives we would be revealing our own magnanimity'. The film shows a number of patients in an institution and comments that looking after them has so far cost 154,000 Marks. 'How many healthy people could have made new homes for themselves abroad with that money?' To house Jewish mental patients 'healthy German citizens must work', the narrator says indignantly; and as the screen shows German girls doing gymnastics, he continues: 'If today we artificially reinstate by humane methods the great law of natural selection, then we shall also be paying respect to the law of the Creator and acknowledging His order.'

The measures taken for the 'preservation of the German race' included a euthanasia programme for the 'incurably sick', the open extermination of undesirable citizens – who included completely healthy opponents of the régime – by means of 'special treatment' as well as experiments designed to facilitate mass sterilisation. At the end of the Polish campaign Hitler assigned full powers to 'Reichsleiter Bouhler and Dr Brandt . . . to extend the authority of certain specifically designated doctors to effect a mercy death on patients who after the most scrupulous investigation of their condition are considered to be in all probability incurably ill.' At the Nuremberg doctors' trials one of the accused – Victor Brack, Bouhler's chief assistant – stated that Bormann had said that euthanasia would 'by no means remain restricted to incurable mental patients', and that from the first Bouhler had reckoned on a misapplication of the terms of the decree. Brack – who played a leading part in the programme of exterminating 'worthless lives' which was carried out under cover of camouflaged organisations like the 'Reich Commission on Welfare and Convalescent Institutions', the 'Public Association of Convalescent Homes' and the 'Public Invalid Transportation Co. Ltd.' – and Brandt, the euthanasia programme chief, suggested that a film should be made to per-

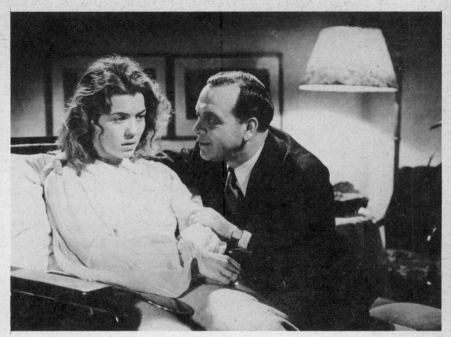

The death scene in *Ich klage an* (Heidemarie Hatheyer, Paul Hartmann)

suade the public to accept euthanasia. The story was contributed by the Chief Medical Officer Wagner's press representative, Hellmuth Unger, who had written a novel called *Mission and Conscience*. The film, directed by Wolfgang Liebeneiner in 1941, was called *Ich klage an* (*I Accuse*) – the accused in this case being a legal system which withheld from doctors the right to make a life or death decision, protected those weaklings who were 'unfit to live', and granted the right to live to others besides those whom Hitler called the 'vigorous majority'.

I Accuse glosses over the genuine dilemma of euthanasia. The central character is a woman suffering from an incurable disease, multiple sclerosis, who pleads with two doctors to put an end to her suffering: a friend, who refuses her request, and her husband, who gives her her 'death on demand'. The victims of the actual euthanasia programme not only did not request their deaths but were murdered against their will and without respect to the wishes of their relatives. Their anonymous and generally merciless deaths were of course in no way comparable to the scene in the film in which the sick woman is given her fatal dose, which makes her 'happier than I have been for a long time' as she hopes that 'this is death'. While the friend who wanted to prolong her life against her will sits in the next room playing Beethoven on the grand piano, her husband tells her, 'Yes, this is death, Hanna.' To which she answers, 'I *do* love you, Thomas.'

In his evidence at the Limburg euthanasia trial on 8 July 1964, and in a tape-recorded interview he gave me in Zürich on 28 March 1965, Liebeneiner said a number of things about the origins of the film. He maintained that Brack showed him the 'Führer's decree' about euthanasia, which prescribed 'mercy killing' only for those who were 'in all probability incurably ill'; and he said that Brack intended to use the film to test public reaction to a law legalising euthanasia. Liebeneiner's starting point in his narrative treatment was a woman suffering from an incurable disease who asks two doctors to perform a mercy killing. The doctors' conflicting opinions were to provide the basis for the film's debate. Brack approved the idea, but later indicated that they would first have to make a film which justified the killing of the mentally ill. 'Somebody put together a script about the imbecile son of a factory foreman and how the child's mother takes special care of him. The foreman kills his son, which leads to a kind of public tribunal – I can't remember it exactly, but anyway it was a fairly ghastly story and they pestered us with it until 1944.' Liebeneiner managed to get the project delayed, and finally it was dropped. But he used the story of the mentally handicapped child to whom death is a kinder fate than life as a subplot in his film, in order to explain why the doctor who refuses to 'help' the sick woman later changes his mind. The doctor '*fought* for the life of this child, and when the little creature didn't want to go on living, I gave him injections and *forced* his heart to go on beating.' He saves the child's life 'for the mother's sake', but she knows no gratitude and accuses him of merely prolonging the child's suffering.

The evidence given by this doctor in the witness box, when he testifies that his friend is no murderer, is one of the highlights of the film's trial sequence, with everyone concerned to secure the acquittal of the man who at her own request has given his wife 'release'. At the end of the film the husband attacks 'the representatives of outmoded opinion and antiquated law': 'This case concerns not just me but hundreds of thousands of hopeless sufferers whose lives we are obliged to prolong unnaturally and whose agonies we thereby increase beyond the bounds of nature ... And it concerns those millions of healthy people to whom we deny protection against illness because all our facilities are used to preserve the substance of life in those to whom death would be a release and to humanity the lifting of a burden.' This quotation comes from the script; in both versions of the film which I have seen this final speech is shorter. Again, the opening scene – a discussion between the jury members during an interval in the trial – which later became the subject of

The euthanasia debate: the jury scene in *Ich klage an*

numerous debates among those responsible for the euthanasia programme – is different in the script from the two versions of the film known to me, which also differ from each other. In the script and in one version of the film, the sentence about it being equally improper to prolong a patient's life artificially as to shorten it artificially is missing. (The whole scene as it appears in the script is reproduced in the appendix to this book.)

The demagogic tactic of ostensibly debating arguments opposed to one's own opinion while actually weakening them by putting them into the mouths of unconvincing spokesmen who merely supply cues to the inevitable winner of the debate is here quite shamelessly applied. The Christian attitude is characterised in a way which allows it to be disposed of immediately as cruel, though of course God Himself is not as cruel as His representatives on earth. The forester on the jury reminds the others that old dogs are put down 'and anyone who doesn't put them down is a brute and no true hunter'. In the script, when someone objects that he is talking about animals, the forester answers that there is no difference between men and animals when it comes to enduring pain. In both versions of the film he asks whether men should have to suffer more than animals. The Major claims that if the State requires death as a duty it should also allow it as a right, adding that there should be a change in the law, which ought not to exist 'if it stops men acting decently and with dignity'.

Here the film has moved far from the reality which it expected its audience to confront. (Its effect on audiences is documented in the Security Service report printed in the appendix.) And wherever film propaganda for euthanasia and the final solution of the Jewish question simulates an apparently documentary reality, what seems to be a straightforward reproduction of reality provides no evidence of what actually happened. The executioners lurk behind the scenes, and there is no mention of the fact that the people destined to die neither wanted their fate nor can be blamed for it.

7. And on to England

The cinema of the Third Reich reflects every phase in relations between the National Socialist state and Great Britain. It is a love–hate relationship, initially displaying signs of admiration and envy. It was only in the last years of the war that the frustrated anger and disillusionment of the rejected suitor was unequivocally voiced. At first Britain is seen as a model. Imperial Germany is criticised for its failure to win colonies when the time was right, as Britain had done, and so establish itself as a real world power; the British are to be emulated. In films with First World War themes, the Englishman is usually a brave, chivalrous opponent. He can't be blamed for using a stratagem of war, as in a film like *Dawn* – this is the only way Germany can be defeated. In the 1934 films with British themes – for instance, Paul Wegener's *Ein Mann will nach Deutschland* (*A Man Wants to go to Germany*) and Herbert Selpin's *Die Reiter von Deutsch-Ostafrika* (*The Riders of German East Africa*) – military service is a depressing but necessary duty which neither the German nor the British patriot can shirk. They are enemies against their will, and enemies who respect each other. The British prison camp commander in *A Man Wants to go to Germany* regards his duty as being unworthy of an officer. Just as sympathetically drawn are the hero's English friend in *The Riders of German East Africa* and the English pilot in Johannes Meyer's *Henker, Frauen und Soldaten* (*Hangmen, Women and Soldiers*, 1935).

British prison camp in *Ein Mann will nach Deutschland*

1935, the year of the German naval pact with Britain, saw homage paid to Britain, in Gerhard Lamprecht's *Der höhere Befehl* (*The Higher Order*), as Prussia's ally against Napoleon and so a defender of European freedom. The English lord and the Prussian cavalry officer are allies in the fight against the French usurper. The fact that Russia also numbered among Prussia's allies in this war of freedom is passed over in the film because of the Franco-Soviet alliance against Hitler.

In Karl Ritter's *Verräter* (*Traitor*, 1936) the British Secret Service is the main opponent of German rearmament. But the film makes a clear distinction between the British patriot who spies for his country and his German associates who betray theirs. Helmut Käutner's *Kitty und die Weltkonferenz* (*Kitty and the World Conference*, 1939) has a British diplomat as a complete master of every finesse in the political game, right up to the happy end. A fact which caused the film to be banned after the outbreak of war.

A film like *The Rothschilds*, made in 1940 during the air-raids on London, combined anti-semitism with an anti-British bias. By this time the British are tools of the Jews. The gallant hero from the other side is now a cowardly plutocrat who lets others do the fighting for him. In *The Rothschilds*

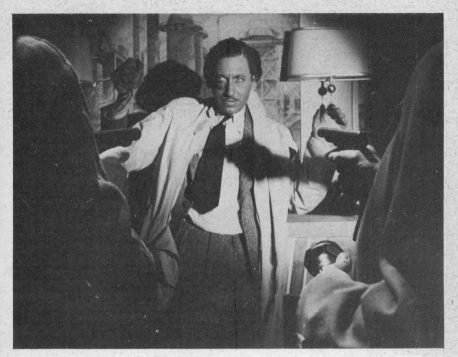

British spy unmasked in *Verräter* (Willy Birgel)

Wellington is portrayed as a corrupt hedonist who leaves the Prussians in the lurch in the struggle against Napoleon. Of course the 'true facts' cannot be proclaimed on the streets with impunity, as young Lieutenant Clayton discovers: he is imprisoned and finally leaves the country where 'God is a business partner' and a free man cannot 'live'. All the same, the film draws a distinction between a British banker and a Jewish banker. There may be an unpleasant John Bull caricature of a British stock exchange speculator, but Nathan Rothschild has a valiant opponent in the incorruptible financier who is eventually ruined by him and who, as a victim of the Jews, seems only to be waiting for a Hitler to liberate the British island race from Jewish domination.

Two films by Max W. Kimmich, *The Fox of Glenarvon* (1940) and *Mein Leben für Irland* (*My Life for Ireland*, 1941), honour the Irish struggle for freedom against the British. The British are here brutal oppressors, unscrupulous in their methods but no match for the hard-headed Irish. The figure of Sir George Beverley in *My Life for Ireland* is characteristic. This wily intriguer, a major in the First War, simply abandoned his Irish sergeant on the battlefield with a bullet in his thigh. To save his own precious life, he

Irish patriot in *Mein Leben für Irland* (Anna Dammann, Werner Hinz)

even took the last water canteen, an action which won him the Victoria Cross for bravery in the face of the enemy. During lessons at an English boarding school, where the sons of Irish revolutionaries are supposed to be turned into proper English gentlemen, the teacher says things like, 'When you appreciate the profound significance of the British right to sovereignty over other nations – that is, her civilising mission – and when you act accordingly, it will be then that you will lead a free and happy life'; and, 'Britain's colonial policy has from the start been governed by the great Christian principle of love of one's fellow-men; even if on occasion she has used force, relentless force, this has happened only when immature peoples opposed measures which were only for their own good.'

Anti-British film propaganda got cruder as Hitler's hopes of a separate peace treaty with Britain receded. By 1941, in films like Herbert Selpin's *Carl Peters* and Hans Steinhoff's *Ohm Krüger*, British colonial power is characterised in terms of the crudest clichés. Though in *Carl Peters*, the British are still cleverer than the short-sighted German bureaucrats. When Peters finds himself no longer supported in his colonial policies by Imperial Germany, the British try to win him over to their side – a proposal which he naturally rejects.

Ohm Krüger is meant to show that 'Britain is the brutal enemy of any kind of order or civilisation'. Ohm Krüger, who rules the Boers like a father, is here the great leader who sees through the wiles of British diplomats and gold-diggers and arms his people in time for the 'final conflict' with Britain. The British can justify any method they use against him. One scene, identical in its effect on an audience to the montage of rats and Jews in *The Wandering Jew*, shows a church service at which the British chaplains distribute arms to the Africans. As the *Illustrierter Filmkurier* put it: 'When England realises that even with cannon and rifles she cannot crush the little nation whose heroic struggle is jubilantly acclaimed by the whole world, she decides to commit one of the most obscene acts in the history of the world.' The technique makes it possible to reveal that concentration camps were no German invention; the peculiar logic of a Goebbels thereby justifies the Nazi camps.

A new general, Kitchener, is assigned the command of the South African war. His methods, which *Ohm Krüger* brands as monstrous, bear a grotesque resemblance to the programme of total war which Hitler promised for the annihilation of British cities. Kitchener observes that his predecessor made a crucial error in respecting 'certain military conventions' which 'may be applicable in normal circumstances but are misplaced in Africa'. So he demands 'an end to woolly humanitarianism, which means hitting the Boers only where they are vulnerable. We must burn their farms, separate wives and children from their menfolk and put them in concentration camps. From

(above and opposite) *Ohm Krüger*: the British concentration camp; after Eisenstein; Victoria as witch

today all Boers, without exception, are outlaws. No distinction is to be made between soldiers and civilians.'

We are shown one of the British concentration camps. The commandant, a caricature of Churchill, appears in one scene which is modelled on a key episode in Eisenstein's *Battleship Potemkin*. Like the sailors in the Eisenstein film who refuse to eat rotten meat, the women in the camp protest against the food they are given. In *Potemkin* the little ship's doctor dons his pince-nez and announces that the maggots are 'dead fly larvae' which can be washed off; in *Ohm Krüger*, the despised authorities are again embodied in a little doctor with a pince-nez, but here the women's revolt is nipped in the bud. If one disregards echoes in Ucicky's *Refugees* of the Odessa Steps sequence in *Battleship Potemkin*, and traces of Eisensteinian visual composition in Leni Riefenstahl's films, this is the only sequence in Nazi cinema which takes up the Propaganda Minister's suggestion that Eisenstein's work was to be taken as a model.

As a leader figure, Ohm Krüger 'doesn't give a damn about the international rights principle'. The film, made forty years after the Boer War, has him called before the tribunal of 'world history' to talk about the day of reckoning: 'Great and powerful nations will resist the British tyranny,

Ohm Krüger: blind prophet (Emil Jannings)

and then the way will be clear for a better world.' Krüger belongs among those who 'make world history'. Not one of the British characters in the film can match his stature. The Queen of England is a crafty old witch who tells her Colonial Minister that the British have not a friend in the world – 'People call us robbers.' On her death-bed she announces: 'The day countries stop hating each other England is lost.' Old Krüger, who had been forced to yield to the superior power of the British, is now a blind prophet; from his exile in Switzerland he issues a warning directed at more than just the German public: 'There can be no coming to terms with the British.'

In a film like Fritz Kirchhoff's *Anschlag auf Baku* (*Attack on Baku*, 1942) the point is made that wherever there is trouble the British have a hand in it. Max W. Kimmich's *Germanin* (1943) paints the British in even blacker colours than *Ohm Krüger*. Here the German drug for sleeping sickness, 'Bayer 205', is rated as superior to all other medicines for the disease. Aschenbach, a German professor whose research station in the jungle had been destroyed by the British at the start of the 1914 war, works on the drug during the war and in 1923 makes an expedition to Africa to combat sleeping sickness. The British see his activities as a threat to their own position, and stop him helping sick Africans. He is ordered to leave Africa, and supplies of his drug 'Germanin' are destroyed. But one ampule survives the destruction; and although Aschenbach himself has contracted sleeping sickness, he cures his arch-enemy the British colonel, who is also suffering from the disease, which gets him permission to clear the jungle and begin an intensive campaign against the tsetse fly. The contrast the film makes between the arrogant, ruthless agents of perfidious Albion and the German scientist who unselfishly sacrifices his own life to give health to Africans [*sic*] is designed to persuade even unsophisticated audiences about which country is really fit for colonial power.

The central scene in *Carl Peters* demonstrates Nazi propaganda's concept of British imperialism as the most dangerous threat to German colonial ambitions. Addressing a parliamentary commission of inquiry in the uniform of an Imperial German *Reichskommissar*, Carl Peters argues for a Hitlerian policy of territorial conquest and emphasises that 'the way the world has been divided up from the 15th century to the present day has left Germany empty-handed'; now she must win colonies. 'Of course territory is not won at round table conferences; territory is only won by men who are hard-headed and self-confident, men who don't wet their pants the moment an Englishman raises his eyebrows.' Like so many of the solitary, uniformed hero figures of Nazi cinema, this pioneer of the German colonial ideal risks a clash with his superiors in his obedience to the call of a higher order. Officially forbidden to

Types of colonialism in *Germanin*: the arrogant British . . .

make comments which might damage the good relations between Britain and Germany, Peters answers that no one can stop him acting 'in the German *interest*'. All means for the protection of that interest are fully sanctioned. Using arguments that might have come from SS officers from the occupied territories after the fall of the Reich, Peters defends himself against the accusation that men were shot without trial on his orders and that 'by his irresponsible actions he damaged the reputation of the German people in the eyes of the whole civilised world'.

It is no accident that both of the *Reichskommissar*'s opponents in this scene are Jews, a high-ranking civil servant and a Social Democrat MP. According to Nazi propaganda, the fight against men of Peters' calibre was led – in Britain as well as Germany – by Jews and their henchmen; and by the end the blond hero has been made a victim of the world Jewish conspiracy. The Jews ask Peters how he can talk of peace when he had hanged people, adding that they themselves would never have countenanced this. To which Peters replies: 'True enough, *you* would never have done it. And *you* wouldn't have won German East Africa either. In any case, if I hadn't had those two Africans hanged on the spot as a deterrent, the rebellion you were plotting would have broken out there and then and hundreds of decent German

... and the beneficent German

farmers would have been massacred. Should I have put in a request to Berlin first? Or maybe I should have asked you or *Vorwärts*?'*

Peters' argument does not prevail; parliament has not yet succumbed to the Führer principle. 'Many dogs are the death of the hare.' With tears in his eyes he exclaims, 'Poor Germany, you are your own worst enemy.' But there is one consolation for him. On his return from this stormy committee session his mother greets him with 'You are *my* little Carl, however much they shout you down and trample over you – come home and don't be sad.' And Peters is sure of himself: 'My ideas, my colonies, they can't trample on them, mother. When we two and those men in there are no more, there'll still be a mountain in Africa 18,000 feet high – Kilimanjaro, the eternal symbol of German East Africa.'

Compared with this British dreams are the dreams of shopkeepers, says the anti-British propaganda film. As early as 16 June 1940 Goebbels had described the island people in terms amply illustrated by the inflammatory anti-British films. For Goebbels, the British 'with their blend of ruthlessness, mendacity, pious hypocrisy and sanctimonious holiness are the Jews among Aryans.'

* Newspaper of the Social Democrat opposition.

8. Honour Your German Masters

In his *Reflections on Film-making*, Dr Fritz Hippler, the Reich script adviser, wrote: 'The one essential requirement for a historical film is that it should have authenticity on a grand scale. The only possible subjects for a successful historical film are personalities and events from the past which people of today know about or can identify with, be interested in or find relevant. To put it in the broadest terms, this is as it were proof of the meaning of life, the authority and historical significance, the timeless authenticity of particular historical events, situations and personalities.' For Hippler the great man of history is the embodiment of a 'life-giving ideal' and as such must also be 'inestimable in human terms'. Third Reich historical films were consistently geared to the times in which their audiences lived. The great poets, painters, sculptors, scientists, explorers, politicians and generals honoured in Third Reich cinema were all projections of the Führer, himself exalted in propaganda as a great general, supreme politician, artist and architect of genius.

The historical films of the period were generally lavishly staged. The subject matter was freely borrowed from primary school textbooks. Every victory in battle is seen as the achievement of a single great man, the fact that generals need soldiers to win their battles being frequently overlooked. In Liebeneiner's *Bismarck*, for example, the Prussian victory at Königgrätz is

Visionaries: Werner Krauss in *Paracelsus*

pictured as a chess game in which all the moves are made according to
General Moltke's calculations. There is not a soldier to be seen in the film;
only the hill from which the King, Bismarck and his generals conduct the
battle. When the King asks Moltke whether he has any orders ready in the
event of a retreat, Moltke replies, 'There will be no retreat here — we are
fighting for Prussia!' Offering the 'great man of few words' his cigar case,
Bismarck is relieved to observe that Moltke calmly chooses the best cigar,
and remarks to the King, 'He seems pretty sure of the situation.' Shortly
afterwards Moltke congratulates the King on his victory.

    The heroes of *Ohm Krüger* and *Carl Peters* belong to the tradition of great
Teutonic figures whose vision and fighting spirit, as it appears in these Nazi
films, characterises them as forbears of Hitler. G. W. Pabst's 1943 film
Paracelsus tells the strange story of the physician who was 'far in advance' of
his age. The portrait of this mysterious, demonic surgeon is intended to
suggest a parallel with Hitler. In 1940, the year of the victory in the West,
appeared a film with the subtitle 'Triumph of Genius'. The hero of this
Herbert Maisch film, the poet Friedrich Schiller, is 'with prophetic certainty'
imbued with the notion that 'there is something more important than the

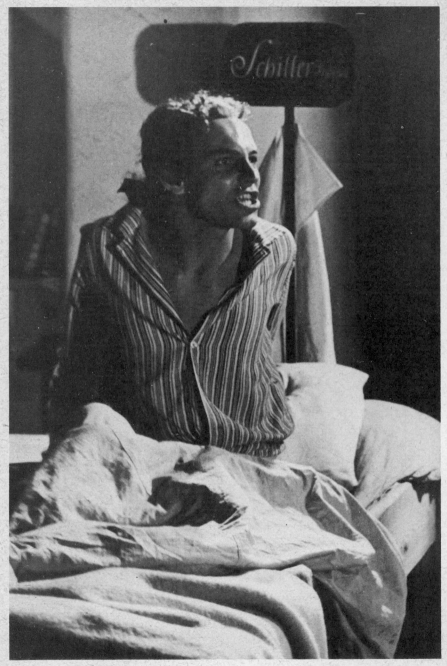

Horst Caspar in *Friedrich Schiller*

rotten politics of the age – greater and nobler than the complacent despotism of petty principalities and their moribund rulers. And this greater ideal which he believed in and for which he fought was one Germany, one people, one fatherland.'

The clash between the young poet and the Duke of Württemberg is seen as a conflict between the genius who needs freedom to fulfil himself and the slavish obedience on which the Duke's rule is founded. A superficial observer might be tempted to see the film as an appeal for freedom of opinion, a protest against the suppression of free speech in the Third Reich. But the film does not align itself against the Duke, who 'probably cannot be blamed for being unable to think beyond the limits of his time'; he is a ruler who rightly demands of his subjects the utmost discipline. Schiller, on the other hand, is the genius, the spiritual leader to whom ordinary laws do not apply. The author of *Robbers* is a forbear of the writer of *Mein Kampf*. He is a superman, whose 'great spirit' – as the *Illustrierter Filmkurier* predictably described it – 'knows no fear and can never comprehend the meanness and pettiness of human caprice'. Schiller leaves 'the homeland which had given him so much happiness and so much torment, and which thus perhaps enabled his genius to mature more swiftly, a genius whose voice he now heard resounding inside him with superhuman force.' Who could fail to be reminded here of the moment when Hitler received his call and decided to go into politics?

After *Friedrich Schiller*, Herbert Maisch made a film about the sculptor and architect *Andreas Schlüter* (1942). Schlüter designs his statue of the great Elector as a monument to a military commander with his eye on the future. He builds a new Berlin, as Hitler designed a new Germany; a giant of town planning whose Berlin, unlike Paris, is modelled on the spirit of ancient Rome. He is resolute, even though the time 'and its people' are against him. Life and art are one and the same to him: 'As long as the one is great and strong, so is the other.' He is what he is, since 'even God can't change that'. He knows only one option – all or nothing. And the moral of the film is, 'You can't build on poor ground', or, 'Life is short, but art is eternal.'

In similar vein 'Robert Koch, who fought death', in Hans Steinhoff's 1939 film, is inspired by a conviction which is 'unshakeable, even though the small minds all around us cannot understand it, or worse, do not want to understand it'. Koch attacks bacteria like a general going to war: 'Where's the enemy hiding, what does he look like, what weapons do I need to fight him?' When Koch eventually 'falls', he is able to 'hand over my weapons to those who come after us. The fight has started and won't be over until the enemy is defeated.' Koch is a leader who requires absolute faith in his mission. He tells his wife: 'No, you don't understand me because you don't believe in me. Or

Heinrich George in *Andreas Schlüter*

do you believe in me?' Koch rebels against the international medical establishment, whose representative, Virchow, typically fails to recognise Koch's importance as a medical authority, just as he refuses to admit Bismarck's greatness as a politician.

The clashes between Virchow and Koch and Virchow and Bismarck illustrate the parallels between the revolutionary scientist and the Iron Chancellor. When Virchow is defeated by Bismarck in a Reichstag debate, Koch tells him in the corridor, 'The medical world is facing a revolution. I am only its instrument.' In the lecture hall at the University, Koch's fight against tuberculosis is hailed as 'a victory for an unwavering belief in an acknowledged mission'. 'The achievement of this man is a valuable and unmistakable guarantee that he was chosen by fate to go on working for the benefit of mankind.' Koch's last speech is an appeal to 'the young people who listen to him with conviction' (as the *Illustrierter Filmkurier* put it); and nothing must prevent them following their duty through to the end. 'You young people will understand me when I say that without sacrifice there can be no life and no progress towards a great objective. I know that these great and good ideas will live on in you, in your minds and in your young hearts. When the torch falls from our hands, you will pick it up again and carry it forward to a new and more glorious day.'

The debate between Bismarck and Virchow was continued in Liebeneiner's *Bismarck*. And with it we may pass from Hitler's forbears to his direct prototypes.

9. The Hitler Prototype

Among the films of 1942 were Veit Harlan's *Der grosse König* (*The Great King*) and Wolfgang Liebeneiner's *Die Entlassung* (*The Dismissal*). That the heroes of these two films, Frederick the Great and Bismarck, were projections of Hitler is underlined in an article by Emil Jannings, who played Bismarck in *The Dismissal*, entitled 'Bismarck in our time'. Jannings reveals that reading Bismarck's speeches he was 'electrified' by a passage which gave him 'an entirely new perspective on the great man'. 'Socialism,' said Bismarck, 'is not an international but a national concern. The State, as the agency best equipped to raise money, must take control. We must aspire to a German state socialism – but directed from above and not under pressure from the streets.' Jannings draws a historical line 'from Frederick the Great to Bismarck to Hitler' and adds: 'This is the right perspective, since in fact these three names represent the same historical situation – one man against the world.'

There had been films about Frederick the Great before the Nazi seizure of power, in which the Prussian king was represented as a symbol of a military strength and discipline which had been lost. On 3 February 1933, just four days after Hitler was made Chancellor of the Reich, there was the first showing of *Der Choral von Leuthen* (*The Hymn of Leuthen*), a film on Frederick directed by Carl Froelich, in which 'old Fritz is not a character from sentimental operetta but the tough soldier of popular imagination and legend', as the film was described during a conversation between the director and the leading player, Otto Gebühr. The film's Frederick was seen by Oskar Kalbus as a man 'possessed by demonic powers of determination'. He takes the road which leads 'either to success or to ruination', thus illustrating 'a highly topical concept of our leader-minded times'.

Hans Steinhoff's *Der alte und der junge König* (*The Old King and the Young King*, 1935) illustrates the transition from young, pleasure-loving Crown Prince to austere King. A year later Johannes Meyer's *Fridericus* presents the Seven Years War in a way which makes Hitler seem like Frederick the Great's legitimate heir. As the film's prologue has it: 'Encircled by European powers who are holding on to rights they regard as hereditary, Prussia is in the ascendant after decades of fighting for the right to exist. The whole world watches with astonishment and admiration as the Prussian King, whom they had first laughed at, then learned to fear, stands his ground in the face of overwhelmingly superior enemy forces. But now they are intent on crushing him. Prussia's hour of destiny has come.' This text includes many of the terms which were to be constantly repeated in the years to come: the fight for *Lebensraum*, Germany's 'encirclement', the admired 'Führer' figure, first mocked, then feared as he confronts superior forces and seizes power in his 'hour of destiny'.

The extent to which the Prussian king's style reflects the language of Nazi cinema can be illustrated by the following quotations. Frederick announces that he 'loves war for its glory', commenting after the Rossbach victory: 'Now they will be talking all over the world of how twenty thousand Prussians defeated fifty thousand Frenchmen and Germans. Now I can lie in my grave in peace because the glory and honour of my people has been saved. We may yet be unlucky, but we are no longer without honour.' An advertising brochure for *The Great King* quoted Frederick as follows: 'The year will be hard and difficult, but we must keep our heads up, and every man who loves and honours his country must stake his all.' In an essay entitled 'History and Film', Harlan wrote that in *The Great King* he had tried 'to bring credibility to the character of the King. I avoided any kind of heroic pose, since I wanted to show the harassed face of a man who after his defeat had almost collapsed under the weight of the responsibility he had shouldered.' It was not Harlan's intention merely to repeat popular anecdotes, but to show the King 'as I think he was — as he must have been'.

The Great King was so clearly modelled on Hitler that he had a print made and sent to Mussolini. The Propaganda Minister issued instructions that reviews of the film should in all circumstances avoid making comparisons between Frederick the Great and Hitler and drawing 'any analogy with the

Der grosse König: 'Führer, command . . .

present, particularly with respect to the pessimistic mood which frequently dominates the commentary at the beginning of the film and which in no circumstances is to be identified with the attitude of the German people in the present war.'

The setting is Prussia after the defeat at Kunersdorf in 1759. Half the Prussian army has been killed in the battle; the whole of the King's entourage considers the situation hopeless and wants peace at any price. But all turns out well in the end. The King survives an assassination attempt – in Nazi films men like Bismarck and Frederick the Great are thanks to providence immune from the assassin's hand. Frederick wins the battle of Torgau, and the Russian Empress' sudden death turns the Russians from enemies into allies. The alliance is short-lived, since the new Tsar is murdered, but the Russians stay in the King's camp for three days, during which he wins the decisive battle against the Austrians. While Prussia celebrates the victory, the King rides back to Kunersdorf, where he had suffered his worst defeat. 'And new life awakens at this scene of horror.' The end of the film is a vision of a Germany which has won the Second World War and is recovering from its exertions. The King is 'deeply moved and profoundly grateful', and enveloped

'. . . we will obey'

by a loneliness for which there is no relief. His life now belongs only to Prussia, just as Hitler was officially wedded only to Germany.

A number of key scenes in the film make direct reference to Hitler. The Army High Command was not overjoyed by the scene in which Frederick takes over the supreme command from Count Fink and continues the war against his generals' wishes. 'Those who are afraid can go home,' contemptuously remarks this 'greatest general of all time' and prototype of Hitler. The King calls 'tradition' an excuse for arrogance. Like Hitler, he expects no privileges as regards food and does without sleep. He wears his tattered Order of the Black Eagle, as Hitler wore his Iron Cross. In one episode he foreshadows Hitler directly. The Bernburg regiment loses its standard and is stripped of its stripes and insignia because at Kunersdorf it 'preferred life to victory'. Colonel Bernburg shoots himself, and the King's comment on his suicide is: 'As he ran away from the battle, he ran away from life.' After the failure of the last great offensive launched by the 6th SS Panzer Division in Hungary, Field Marshal Keitel sent a telegram to SS Group Commander Sepp Dietrich: 'The Führer thinks that the troops did not fight as the situation demanded, and therefore orders the SS Divisions Adolf Hitler, the Reich, the

Death's Head and the Hohenstaufen to remove their stripes [together with their embroidered Division names].'

The Bernburg regiment also features in Karl Ritter's *Cadets*, made in 1939 but because of its anti-Russian line not released until 1941. A cavalry officer, who has not forgiven the King for the punishment meted out to the regiment, deserts to the Russian lines to avenge the King's insult in asking the regiment to defend a hopeless position. He has promised himself that the King will get to know his name 'and will have to say to himself that this is one of the Kunersdorf officers whom I demoted because they did their duty'. But this rebellious officer returns to the Prussian side to help the Potsdam cadets, who have been carried off by the Russians but have managed to escape. He leads them in the attack against the pursuing Russians and makes good his betrayal of the Prussians by dying a hero's death. The film thus passes judgment on the subject who insists on his rights. The King alone decides what is right.

There is also a rebel in *The Great King* – Sergeant Treskov, whose action decides the battle of Torgau. General Ziethen is to attack on a given signal. When the signal is not given and the sergeant sees that his regiment is in danger, he gives it himself on no authority. The King promotes him to officer rank, and orders him to be bound to the wheel for three days for showing lack of discipline. Treskov does not understand the King's attitude and decides to desert, only to be killed in the next battle. His crime was his unthinking insolence in assuming that an insignificant sergeant could take the initiative instead of doggedly obeying orders. Like the cavalry officer in *Cadets*, there is only one way for him to atone for his sin – he must die for Prussia.

In his diary, Goebbels comments on the success of *The Great King*, which was awarded the 'Film of the Nation' citation. 'The film works extremely well as political education. We need this today. We live in a time which could do with some of Frederick's spirit. The difficulties confronting us can only be mastered if we stretch ourselves to the utmost. If we can overcome them, we shall undoubtedly stiffen our national resistance; and here again what Nietzsche said holds good – experience that does not break us can only make us stronger.' On the protest of the generals at headquarters against the film's suggestion that Frederick the Great had been left in the lurch by his generals in his hour of need, Goebbels writes: 'It's strange. The gentlemen at the Foreign Office feel themselves responsible for every mistake in foreign policy in the last hundred years; the gentlemen at the Army High Command feel guilty about every bit of general staff inertia, even if it happened in the Seven Years War.' Goebbels considers this 'as short-sighted as it is foolish' and notes that Keitel was very taken with the film and managed to calm the disaffected general staff. He also remarks that the film provides an extremely vivid picture of 'the solitude in which the Führer lives and works today', and

Bismarck (Hans Junkermann, Paul Hartmann)

that *The Great King* was released at just the right moment 'to give additional weight to the gradual introduction of tougher methods in fighting the war'. The Propaganda Minister's diary also reveals 'what a comfort this characterisation of the great king' was to Hitler, who under the influence of the film was very receptive to Goebbels' proposals for intensifying the war effort.

The first of Wolfgang Liebeneiner's two Bismarck films was made at the time of Hitler's rapid and impressive military successes, as he advanced on the Western Front in the steps of the victor at Sedan. The Bismarck of the 1940 film is the newly appointed Prussian Prime Minister who dissolves Parliament when it disobeys him, concludes a military agreement with Russia in order to protect Prussia's rear, and lays the foundations of German unification not by making speeches and following majority decisions but by 'iron and blood'. The greatness of this leader figure is emphasised by the pettiness of his opponents, whose spokesman is Professor Virchow. During a parliamentary session Virchow musters very reasonable arguments against Bismarck, and therefore against Hitler. But the fact that the arguments are his, and that he represents Bismarck, the architect of the German Empire, as an obstacle to the unification of Germany, means that his words lose their force. The dissolution of the Prussian Parliament is preceded by the following exchange between Bismarck and Virchow:

BISMARCK: This has nothing to do with my person or my property. I intend to dissolve this Parliament, which has caused so much disorder, by order of the King until the conflict is resolved and Prussia is out of danger.

VIRCHOW: Sir, you are violating the constitution.

Uproar

MEMBERS: Just who is this Bismarck?

Uproar

BISMARCK: It is not the King who is violating the constitution, gentlemen, it is you – you have already done so. The constitution lays down that laws are passed on the basis of an agreement between Parliament and the King. By your doctrinaire attitude you have made this agreement impossible. So the constitution is suspended. But the machinery of government must continue to function, the trains must run, the Post Office must deal with the mail, the civil servants must draw their salaries and you, gentlemen, your allowances. Who is to look after all this now? You, gentlemen? No, we shall of course have government by the King, who alone has the responsibility, the right and the power for it.

PRESIDENT: The honourable member Virchow has the floor.

VIRCHOW: Gentlemen, this is a black day in our history. In the midst of a struggle for the ideals of liberty and progress, Prussia is thrown back into the darkness of the Middle Ages. Our garden of reason has been turned into a barracks. No, gentlemen, thus far and no further. We are a nation of poets and thinkers, and we are proud of it . . .

BISMARCK: But don't you see the irony in the words 'a nation of poets and thinkers'? While you sit here dreaming, others are dividing the world between them!

VIRCHOW: I beg you not to interrupt me. We do not want the world, we want freedom in our country.

BISMARCK: But you haven't got that either; the others have got it. There is one country between Calais and Marseilles, and six frontiers between Hamburg and Munich.

VIRCHOW: The unity of heart and spirit is superior to any decree. This unity has already been achieved ...

BISMARCK (*to Roon*): German Michael has to be *forced* to accept his good fortune.

VIRCHOW: Herr von Bismarck and Herr von Roon may smile at my words. They are men for whom, in the President's words, might is stronger than right.

BISMARCK: I did not say that might is stronger than right. Don't twist my words.

VIRCHOW: This is not a question of words but of facts. Herr von Bismarck and Herr von Roon are enemies of the people, devoid of patriotism. But I will assure you of one thing, and I want it recorded by history now. A certain Herr von Bismarck will not succeed in preventing the unification of Germany.

The way in which the sentence 'We do not want the world, we want freedom in our own country', in itself rather surprising in a Third Reich context, is here rendered innocuous is characteristic of the demagogic tactics of the period. Audiences are given no opportunity to dwell on the concept of freedom. Virchow is immediately interrupted by Bismarck, and before the audience has had time to indulge in undesirable thoughts, freedom is being equated with tourist traffic unhampered by border controls. Instead of returning to freedom, Virchow puts a unity of 'heart and spirit' above the principles of federalism – and Bismarck demolishes his whole speech with the superior smile of the man of action whose conclusion to a debate of this nature is that 'German Michael', the muddled dreamer, has to be 'forced into accepting his good fortune'. The impotence of the parliamentary 'chat club' is apparent, and the audience is left appreciating that the Führer principle is a prerequisite for the unity and greatness of the Reich. Which was the intention.

The Dismissal, the second of the Bismarck films, is concerned with Bismarck's dismissal which, in Jannings' words, opened the door to 'the political dilettantes he so despised and paved the way to Versailles. For the fate of a nation rests not on its institutions but on its personalities. Anyone who tries to stop them is stopping a country breathing.' The Bismarck who fascinated Jannings announced after he had secured Germany's unification: 'If we stay united, we will form a wedge in the centre of Europe which no one will budge without getting his fingers squashed.' The instrument of this unity was the army, without which Germany 'will not survive. It would neither have existed in the first place nor will it hold out.' To Jannings, Bismarck's Reich is only a partial solution; 'He may have united the German races, but he was

Die Entlassung: Emil Jannings as Bismarck, Werner Hinz as Wilhelm II

unable to provide them with the room that was essential for their strength and vitality.' The great man's dismissal is only brought about by an unscrupulous schemer who, with no responsibilities of his own, exploits the young and inexperienced Kaiser's ambition to guide his country's destiny himself. By the time this film was made Bismarck's legacy had passed to Hitler. The film anchors Hitler's war of conquest in Prussian history – the realisation of Bismarck's policies. *The Dismissal* was also shown under the title *Change of Destiny*, thereby implying that both Bismarck and Hitler acted at the behest of an immutable destiny. The consequence of their struggle is either victory or ruination. And if victory is not allotted to them, it is not their doing but that of destiny, who decided against them, or of the people, who did not deserve them as leaders.

10. Götterdämmerung

'It is up to us whether this war is a curse or a blessing. It demands of us our utmost, but it will also give us everything we need for our future as a nation. Which one of us, given the choice, would exchange these times for other, calmer and therefore less significant times? The day will come when our troubles and anxieties are over, and we too shall hear the bells ringing for the end of the war and for victory. That moment will be the reward for all of us. Every individual will have to account for what he has done and what he has failed to do, and then as a nation we shall go before the tribunal of history. Humbling ourselves before the mighty destiny we have shouldered and mastered, we shall bow our heads to receive the laurel.'

These lines from a speech by Goebbels, along with a quotation from Frederick the Great, appeared on a publicity brochure for *The Great King*. In the course of the war years the Propaganda Minister's rhetorical style was increasingly influenced by historical documents. As early as 1940, at a rally in Münster, he quoted Frederick the Great's motto, 'Praise be to that which hardens a man.' In Nazi films, characters from German history talk like Hitler and Goebbels, and the Third Reich leaders never tired in their efforts to find comfort in the old Prussian king's example and to compare their own situation with the crises which Frederick had overcome. According to Goebbels, the Prussians would have collapsed under the weight of their misfortunes during the Seven Years War 'had not the masterful spirit of their great king continually given them strength'. After Stalingrad, Nazi propaganda kept on hoping for a miracle equal to the death of the Empress Elisabeth during the Seven Years War. Shortly before the final collapse, Roosevelt's sudden death was thought to have given them the analogy they needed. Right up to the end Goebbels endeavoured to persuade the masses to believe in final victory, a tactic designed to keep their fighting spirit from flagging. On 7 January 1945 he wrote: 'A people of honour should not rest on its laurels. The laurel wreath is wound round the head leaf by leaf, won by noble endurance, fighting spirit and heroic courage, until it forms a full crown round the gallant brow.' A few weeks later, on 30 January 1945, the twelfth anniversary of the Nazi seizure of power, the last 'Film of the Nation', Veit Harlan's *Kolberg*, had its première. On 1 June 1943, Goebbels had written to Harlan: 'I hereby commission you to make the epic film *Kolberg*. The film is to demonstrate, through the example of the town which gives it its title, that a people united at home and at the front will overcome any enemy. I authorise you to request whatever help and support you deem necessary from all Army, Government and Party agencies, and you may refer to this film which I have hereby commissioned as being made in the service of our intellectual war effort.'

In his autobiography Harlan recalls that Goebbels ordered him to use the historical events which occurred at Kolberg in 1806 and 1807 and to invent a love story to go with them, as he had already done for his Frederick the Great film. In conversation with Harlan, Goebbels identified himself with Nettelbeck, the mayor of the beleaguered town of Kolberg who called on the population to form a civilian militia and make a stand against Napoleon's army. 'Goebbels saw this civilian militia as a kind of SA. He wanted it emphasised that at least as far as Kolberg was concerned the real hero was Nettlebeck and not the great general Gneisenau.' Without belittling Gneisenau's contribution, Goebbels wanted to show that in the conflict between the Army and the Party organisations it was the latter who came out on top. Although the historical Nettelbeck was a small, thin man, in the film he is a rugged, earthy father figure. The film's aim was to prove that it was the people and not the military who wanted to resist to the last and that 'every Prussian, whether civilian or in uniform, has to be a soldier'. According to Harlan, Hitler wanted Napoleon to have 'an awe-inspiring appearance'; he admired the French emperor because – so Goebbels assured *Kolberg*'s director – he had prevented the Germans from doing away with the whole miserable 'spectre of nationhood' in Europe. 'Now Europe will have to learn to be German.'

Goebbels noted in his diary: 'I expect extraordinary things of this Harlan

Kolberg: Napoleon at the tomb of Frederick the Great

film. It fits exactly the political and military landscape we shall probably have to reckon with by the time the film can be shown.' On the day of the film's première this landscape was the ruins of Berlin and the beleaguered fortress of La Rochelle. A print of *Kolberg* was flown in to La Rochelle, and to mark the first performance Goebbels sent the commandant a telegram: 'The film is an artistic hymn of praise to the courage and endurance which is prepared to make the greatest sacrifice for people and homeland. It will therefore have a worthy opening performance to mark the close ties between those men fighting at the front and at home who are displaying to the whole nation the virtues demonstrated in this film. My wish is that the film will be accepted by you and your courageous soldiers as a document of the unwavering resolution of a people which, in these days of worldwide struggle, united with those fighting at the front, is willing to emulate the great example of its glorious history. *Heil* to our Führer!' The commandant replied: 'Opening performance of colour film *Kolberg* took place today in La Rochelle Theatre for soldiers of all units of defence zone. Deeply moved by the courageous action of the Kolberg fortress and incomparable artistic presentation, we add to our gratitude for the despatch of the film on 30 January our renewed vow to emulate the heroic struggle at home and not to fall short of them in our perseverance and initiative. Long live Germany, long live our Führer!' Shortly afterwards La Rochelle surrendered. The fact that Kolberg fell into Soviet hands while *Kolberg* was running could clearly not be made public. But it was not difficult to read between the lines of the belatedly published news that the fortress commandant had been given the Oak Leaf decoration for the decisive part he '*had* played' in its defence.

While *Kolberg* was shooting, Soviet forces took Kiev and pressed on towards Germany. By October 1944 they had crossed the East Prussian border. The Allies meanwhile took Rome and landed in northern France, entered Paris and Amsterdam and by September 1944 had crossed the western German frontier. While *Kolberg* was shooting, the Hungarian Jews were deported to Auschwitz, the attempt on Hitler's life failed, the German *Volkssturm* was formed, and the German offensive in the Ardennes was launched to halt the Allied advance. As early as December 1943, Harlan had told a press conference that the film 'is intended as a memorial to Gneisenau and Nettelbeck and to the people of Kolberg; but above all it is a memorial to the German people today.'

In reality, the example of Kolberg demonstrates the absurdity of last-ditch resistance propaganda and the horrors of total war. The film's message for the most part rebounds against those who commissioned it. Behind the fustian dialogue one can detect the cynicism of the propagandists, who even went as far as to appeal to religious sentiment. Gone is the time when Goebbels was proudly boasting about his ability to produce invisible propaganda. Addressing the State Film Department in 1941, he had said: 'This is the really great art – to educate without revealing the purpose of the education, so that one fulfils an educational function without the object of that education being in any way aware that it is being educated, which is also indeed the real purpose of propaganda. The best propaganda is not that which is always openly revealing itself; the best propaganda is that which as it were works invisibly, penetrates the whole of life without the public having any knowledge at all of the propagandist initiative.'

Shortly before his death Harlan said in an interview that he had 'no intention of belittling this film in any way or of disparaging its human approach, but it was obvious to everyone who worked on the film and everyone who saw it later why it was made. It was no secret that Goebbels' propaganda had a very specific aim. So the film was propaganda for something which people knew there had to be propaganda about, and it wasn't all that dangerous.' A curious apology for a film which combined the theme 'Now, people, rise, and storm, break out!' from the Wars of Liberation with a demand for total war, and which was aimed at persuading the last surviving civilians to die for Hitler. The speeches in the film are in part verbatim quotations from statements made by Goebbels and other propagandists at *Volkssturm* rallies held while the film was being shot. What the film failed to show was the Führer's attitude to his people.

One of the highlights of *Kolberg* is the moment when Queen Luise, that embodiment of all that is Prussia, grants an audience to a simple Kolberg girl with the symbolic name of Maria. To the accompaniment of melting celestial music the Queen tells the farmer's daughter that she receives daily reports from Kolberg and that Maria can be proud of her home town. She then embraces Maria with the words, 'This is how I take Prussia and Kolberg to my heart. There are only a few jewels left in our crown. Kolberg is one of them.'

Adolf Hitler's attitude was somewhat different. In a speech to his *Gauleiters* in 1944, he remarked that the German people did not deserve to survive if it could not win the war. At Nuremberg, Albert Speer testified that Hitler blamed the German people and not himself for the catastrophe, and insisted that the fight should go on until victory or total destruction. And this order was given at a time when there could no longer be any doubt that defeat was inevitable. During the German retreat the 'scorched earth' policy was now applied to German soil. Hitler intended to take the German people down with him. According to Speer's evidence at Nuremberg, Hitler told him on 18 March 1945: 'When the war is lost the people will also be lost. This fate is inescapable. It is not necessary for us to concern ourselves with the basic essentials the people may need for even a very primitive survival. On the contrary, it would be better to destroy even these. Because the country has proved itself the weaker force, and the future belongs exclusively to the stronger Eastern countries. Anything that survives the fight will in any case be inferior because all the good men have fallen.' Alexander and Margarete Mitscherlich have commented on this attitude of Hitler's in their book *Impossible to Mourn*. Hitler 'embodied the great ideal of a subject population crippled by years of absolute rule, and conversely projected his own great ideal on the "race" factor which was supposed to distinguish the German people'. Hitler regarded the German people as unworthy of him because they had not fulfilled his 'narcissistic ambitions' – 'just as in the end he failed to pluck the stars from heaven, the fantasies of omnipotence which the average, passive, expectant citizen projected on to him.'

The leading characters in *Kolberg* have historical names, and the film's prologue assures us that the story is based on 'historical fact'. The most important parts of the story, however, are wholly invented. In the film the siege of Kolberg comes to a halt because the beleaguered town's stubborn resistance leads to a quarrel between the French generals. One of them wants to take the town at any price, which would earn him the title of 'Duke of Kolberg'; the other is anxious to stop the senseless bloodshed. This kind of quarrel between enemy generals is the miracle on which Nazi propaganda repeatedly staked its hopes. In reality, the French entered Kolberg, and their artillery batteries stopped firing because the attacking forces were informed by a Prussian courier that a truce had been agreed. Gneisenau, the film's young hero, was in fact 47 years old when he commanded the troops at Kolberg. He never entertained any prospect of capitulation, nor was he the author of the proclamation 'To my people', which was signed in 1813 by King Frederick William III. The subplot in which Gneisenau persuades the King to issue this proclamation by describing Kolberg's resistance was added to avoid having the film end with the fall of Kolberg. By referring to the Wars of Liberation which brought about Napoleon's downfall, the film was able to turn defeat into victory.

Gneisenau's predecessor, Colonel Loucadou, is also maligned. The film suggests that this old-style career officer was unwilling to fight, and had Nettelbeck, the town's citizens' representative, arrested and sentenced to death. The historical Loucadou only threatened to do this, and the fighting began when he was in fact still commander at Kolberg. The film makes no mention of the fact that the British came to the town's help. It uses the relationship between Gneisenau and Nettelbeck to show how everyone, even the leader of the militia, has to submit to discipline. 'You want to lead and can't even obey orders' is what in effect Gneisenau says to Nettelbeck, who after refusing to obey what he takes to be a wrong order from Gneisenau finally submits to his commander's directive that no one can simply obey the orders he considers right and sensible: 'Granted you are right in this instance. But does that really matter? That would be the shortest route to anarchy.' Gneisenau 'can only apply the right that is based on law and discipline'. The alternative to obedience at any price is contrasted with chaos. Just as Goebbels, on 4 February 1945, had remarked that the mere thought of defeat for National Socialism conjured up 'visions of European chaos'.

The German people is represented in *Kolberg* by the Werner family. The father sacrifices his farm to the scorched earth policy, lighting the fire himself and perishing in the flames. His son Friedrich, a member of Major Schill's volunteer corps, dies in action. The second son, Klaus, is a caricatured 'man of the world', refusing to join the ranks of the fighting community, irritating the wounded hero Schill by playing the violin, and losing his nerve when he hears the cannon-fire. He is killed by a shell while trying to save his violin from an already evacuated house. His sister Maria, the family's sole survivor, is in love with Schill in a timid, devoted kind of way; as her hero sails off to new wars, she is left behind on the shore. When the siege is over, Nettelbeck

Kolberg: Nettelbeck (Heinrich George) and Maria (Kristina Söderbaum)

salutes her: 'Yes, you gave your all, Maria. But it was not in vain ... Fine things have always come through hardship. And when someone takes the hardship on herself on our behalf, that's a really fine person. You're a fine person, Maria. You stayed in your place, you did your duty, you weren't afraid to die. You helped us to win, Maria, you too!'

Kolberg clearly demonstrates the schizophrenic nature of Nazi propaganda. Did not Hitler in 1940 stand at Napoleon's grave just as the film's Napoleon stands at the grave of Frederick the Great? Did not Hitler in the Europe of his time play Napoleon's role as oppressor of defeated nations? Is there not a resemblance between the images of people in *Kolberg* jumping from their burning homes in a desperate attempt to save themselves and the pictures taken by SS General Stroop in the Warsaw ghetto? The French round-up of peasants and their irritation with the recalcitrant citizens of Kolberg find parallels in Nazi policies during the Second World War. Isn't the glorification of discipline in this devastated town a demonstration of the slavish obedience principle taken to absurd lengths? And doesn't *Kolberg* also unconsciously pay tribute to the resistance to Hitler? What must have gone through the mind of someone watching the film in the embattled fortress of La

(above and opposite) *Kolberg*: propaganda war games

Rochelle or the burning city of Berlin when he heard Gneisenau's final words about the people rising up at last to shake off their chains? 'The people rise, the storm breaks out' – but might not the storm destroy those who unleashed it? 'Phoenix-like from the ashes and the ruins a new people will arise, a new Reich!' Words that in 1945 could scarcely be applied to the Third Reich. And what was being alluded to in the conversation between Gneisenau and the King, the enthusiastic pioneer of the civilian militia idea and the hesitant head of state who asks what the people have to offer him? The film's Gneisenau talks the language of the Propaganda Minister. Is this scene a coded appeal to Hitler, echoing Goebbels' intervention at the Führer's headquarters after the showing of the Frederick the Great film?

The expenditure lavished on *Kolberg* assumed grotesque proportions. Veit Harlan had more troops at his disposal for his war games than did both sides put together during the actual battle for Kolberg. In spite of the enormous supply problems, no expense was spared as far as *Kolberg* was concerned. Press reports on the shooting were vetoed – the enormous amounts spent on the film might well have provoked a public reaction. The total cost amounted to 8½ million Marks. For one scene Charlemagne's Imperial Crown was used.

Harlan recalls that he had 10,000 uniforms made and that he used 6,000 horses. 187,000 soldiers, according to Harlan's own estimate, were withdrawn from active service. The actor who plays Schill in the film was an officer in General Vlassov's Cossack regiment. Several trainloads of salt were used to transform fields and rooftops into a snow-covered landscape. For the sequence of the French attack across flooded fields Harlan asked for 4,000 sailors. The Admiralty refused, but he got them after an appeal to the Propaganda Ministry. In retrospect, Harlan admitted that a 'law of madness' prevailed, and everyone submitted to it though they knew it was madness. 'Hitler as well as Goebbels must have been obsessed by the idea that a film like this could be more useful to them than even a victory in Russia. Maybe they too were now just waiting for a miracle because they no longer believed in victory in any rational way. In the cinema's dream factory miracles happened at home quicker than they did at the front.'

Goebbels was not pleased with *Kolberg*'s sentimental, romanticised 'drawing-room' scenes – to which Harlan still referred with pride in his autobiography – nor with the way the film depicted the horrors of war. He was uncertain how the population would react to a realistic presentation of their own situation dressed up as history. The film was not meant to encourage defeatism. So Goebbels ordered cuts involving sequences which in Harlan's words had described 'for 2 million Marks the horrors of total war'. A memorandum to Goebbels from the then State script supervisor, Hinkel, dated 6 December 1944, includes a list of the changes ordered by Goebbels and approved by Harlan. He promises to deal with them quickly:

1. Cut all the mass battle and street scenes and replace with scenes featuring the familiar characters.
2. Delete the birth scene from the moment when the pregnant woman is brought into the town councillor's house up to the scene following the birth of the child and the removal of mother and child from the house.
3. Cut the hysterical outburst of the brother Klaus.
4. Cut the Queen Louise audience scene by removing one or two close-ups of Frau von Meyendorff and Frau Söderbaum.
5. Cut the argument between Gneisenau and Nettelbeck about the command at Kolberg. Delete the sentence about him (Gneisenau) having sole responsibility.

Hinkel also mentions in this memorandum a scene which in his opinion is 'an even more effective passage from Gneisenau's speech in the market-place' which 'for obvious reasons could be put to excellent use', and which includes among other things sentences like, 'You have lost everything, but you have also won everything ... Germans of every region, take your cue from Kolberg ... I see the dawn of German freedom rising ...'

On Gneisenau's arrival in Kolberg, Nettelbeck is said to have gone down on his knees in front of his new commander. In the film he does this during a conversation which is reminiscent of one of Goebbels' wartime speeches, or of the dialogue between the U-boat commander and his crew in *Dawn*:

GNEISENAU: 35,000 men, Nettelbeck, and at least 500 guns, and all directed against this town. Do you realise what that means? Compared with this, everything we've experienced up to now is child's play.

NETTELBECK: Commander, will you please tell me frankly what you are trying to say.

GNEISENAU: We are finished, Nettelbeck, it's senseless to go on. We cannot hold the town.

NETTELBECK: And?

GNEISENAU: Surrender, Nettelbeck!

NETTELBECK: Oh yes, like Magdeburg, Erfurt, Stettin and Spandau. It was all in vain, then? The end – dishonour?

GNEISENAU: There is no dishonour when soldiers have fired their last bullet. Even Blücher had to capitulate.

NETTELBECK: But, commander, we haven't fired our last bullet. And after all Blücher did not have to surrender the town he was born in. You were not born in Kolberg, Gneisenau. You were ordered to Kolberg. But *we* grew up here. We know every stone, every street corner, every house. So, we won't let go now! And even if we

Kolberg 1807–Germany 1945

have to hang on to the soil of our town with our fingernails, we won't let go. No, they will have to hack our hands off one by one, kill us one after the other. Gneisenau, you can't expect an old man like me to dishonour himself by handing our town over to Napoleon. And I have promised our King, too. Better be buried under the ruins than capitulate. Gneisenau, Gneisenau, I have never gone on my knees to anyone before. Now I'm doing it. Gneisenau, Kolberg must not be surrendered!

GNEISENAU: That is what I wanted to hear from you, Nettelbeck. Now we can die together.

As in *Dawn*, being ready to die a hero's death is all that counts. In the reality of 1945 the miracle that saved Kolberg in the film never happened. But something Nettelbeck says in the film was true for many people: 'And if we can't live as men, then we'll live like mice, like moles.' In the still unoccupied parts of the Reich the film was hardly shown. As the Red Army marched into Guben and Babelsberg, work was still being done on the editing of the second negative. In Breslau and Danzig the film was sent into action, as it were; it was shown to the fighting units and the people of beleaguered cities. Goering, Himmler, Dönitz and Guderian were given copies. The *Völkischer Beobachter* correspondent saw the film's version of Kolberg in 1807 'as if it were part of ourselves', referring to 'its uncanny relevance to our times'. But the catastrophe could not be halted by the film. Hitler evaded responsibility for his actions by committing suicide. Goebbels followed suit. On 17 April 1945, a few days before his death, he told his colleagues at the Propaganda Ministry: 'Gentlemen, in a hundred years time they will be showing a fine colour film of the terrible days we are living through. Wouldn't you like to play a part in that film? Hold out now, so that a hundred years hence the audience will not hoot and whistle when you appear on the screen.'

Only just over twenty-five years have passed since these words were spoken. The hero's role which Goebbels chose for himself has long since lost any credibility it might have had. The myth that under Goebbels' control of German cinema important works of art were created could only persist over the years because so many films of the period were either banned or have been lost. But it is clear that his propaganda did not lose its dangerous powers of suggestion with the collapse of the Third Reich. *Kolberg* was shown in Argentina after the war as *Burning Hearts* and in Switzerland as *The Renunciation*. The *Neue Zürcher Zeitung* commented on the film's 'ostentatious dishonesty' and expressed a hope that the common sense of the Swiss would react 'against this retrospective infiltration of Nazi refuse'. The Zurich *Filmberater*, however, praised the film as 'a hymn to loyalty, but also to Prussianism'. Within the last fifteen years anti-Israeli propagandists have put on *Jud Süss* in the Middle East, and anti-British propagandists have shown

Ohm Krüger in Greece. Only when Nazi propaganda has been exposed for what it is and its content clearly marked can its poison be rendered harmless. It will then reveal itself as a preparation for collective self-sacrifice and self-righteousness, as an invitation to worship power and renounce independent critical judgment in exchange for blind submission to the will of the Führer or of 'Providence'.

This brand of propaganda rejected the notion of objective truth and enlisted a new kind of morality, which enabled Himmler to celebrate mass murder as 'a glorious page in our history'. Words like 'decent', for instance, thus acquired a new meaning. In a speech to SS officers on 4 October 1943 Himmler announced: 'Most of you will know what it means to see a hundred or five hundred or a thousand corpses lying about. To have experienced this and to have remained decent – apart from a few cases of human weakness – this is what has made us tough.' In *Kolberg* a member of the council wants to know 'why we may have to sacrifice ourselves, for what purpose and to what object'. Nettelbeck answers: 'Ah, you need reasons to stay a decent fellow!'

Thus is any opposition to the leadership's claim to absolute rule branded in advance. Here is the unmistakable evidence of what the Nazi propagandists considered their most dangerous enemy: the courage and ability to think for oneself, the unbroken free will of the individual.

Appendix

I: Documents on four films

i **Triumph of the Will**

At a Ufa board meeting on 28 August 1934, a contract was agreed with Leni Riefenstahl, as 'special representative of the National Socialist Party administration', for the German distribution rights of the film *1934 Party Rally* 'exclusively and without limit of time'. The contract included 16mm distribution. The minutes of the meeting state that Hitler had agreed that the film should be distributed by Ufa and that the 'artistic and technical direction of the film' was to be vested with Fräulein Riefenstahl 'who is hereby commissioned by the Führer in the name of the National Socialist Party administration according to a letter dated 19.4.1934'. (Minute no. 1021, Ufa Board Meetings.)

In September 1934 *Das Archiv*, a 'Reference Book for Politics, Economics and Culture', edited by Dr Kurt Jahncke, senior civil servant in the State Propaganda Ministry, and supervised by Ernst Jaenicke, director of the Greater Berlin Area Press Office of the National Socialist Party, included the following entry:

The Party Rally Film

The Führer has chosen *Triumph of the Will* as the title of the major film of the 1934 Party Rally ... Nearly 100,000 metres of film were shot. The first part of the film shows the early history of the movement. This was filmed by Walter Ruttmann, while the Nuremberg material, as in the previous year, was directed by Leni Riefenstahl. The National Socialist Party administration has forbidden the showing of individual records of the Party Rally, other than material produced for the newsreels on the authority of the National Administration.

On 17 August 1934, Leni Riefenstahl wrote to 'Fellow Party Member Karl Auen, Film Association' complaining about a cameraman who had said that it was beneath his dignity to work on the Party Rally film under Leni Riefenstahl's direction. The letter concludes with the observation that she considers this remark 'an expression of disparagement for a work commissioned by the Führer' and with a request for comment on this information. On 29 August she wrote a second letter, in which among other things she said:

... If the Führer does not find it beneath his dignity to entrust me with the artistic direction of this work, it is curious, to say the least, that Herr Schünemann finds it beneath his dignity to acknowledge this. The Führer's commission would be impracticable if other unit members were to take Herr Schünemann's view. It was for this reason that I felt it necessary to inform you of this matter.

In her book *Behind the Scenes of the Party Rally Film*, published in 1935 by Franz Eher, the National Socialist Party's central publishing house, Leni Riefenstahl describes the shooting of *Triumph of the Will*. She begins with the observation, 'My personal involvement in this project overcomes all doubts, all misgivings, all obstacles.' She informs us that she had a unit of 120 personnel at her disposal, including 16 cameramen and 16 assistant operators with 30 cameras, 4 sets of sound equipment, lights, 22 chauffeur-driven cars, SA and SS bodyguards, field police officers and 'in addition 16 newsreel cameramen whose extensive experience was of valuable assistance in the making of the film'. Leni Riefenstahl describes the elaborate preparations for the shooting. One of the iron masts in the Luitpoldhain was fitted with a lift to hoist a cameraman to a height of 125 feet. At the Adolf-Hitler-Platz 65 feet of track were laid at first floor level to facilitate camera movement for overhead shots of the parade. Describing the rallies, she admires 'the enormous strength and resilience of the Führer, as after a strenuous day's work he stands in his car for hours reviewing the parade'. During the Labour Service parade 'the sun disappeared behind the clouds. But the moment the Führer arrives, its rays break through the clouds: Hitler weather!' In her opinion, Hitler 'recognised the importance of the film' and 'once again provided an

Leni Riefenstahl during the filming of *Triumph of the Will*

unprecedented example of how a conviction, once it is recognised as valuable and right, can be realised on a grand scale'. She maintains that 'the belief that a nation can relive a real, important event through the medium of film was born in Germany. Thus the Führer gives the topical film a meaning and a mission.'

In a chapter called 'The Final Version' she comments on the completion of the film:

It is not important to get everything on the screen in the right chronological order. The structural outline demands that one finds the road to unity by instinct, influenced by the real experience of Nuremberg, so that the film takes shape in a way that, scene by scene, impression by impression, makes an overwhelming impact on the viewer and listener.

I try to discover the inner dramatic force of this retrospective structure. It is there. It will communicate itself to the people as soon as the film of Nuremberg has taken shape, as soon as the speeches and the sentences, the mass images and the shots of individual heads, the marching and the music, the pictures of Nuremberg at night and in the morning, have been composed into a symphonic whole which will do justice to the meaning of Nuremberg. The Führer himself coined the title of the film *Triumph of the Will*.

And in doing so he has indicated the meaning the film is to convey.

So from the theme of this exultant title there rises a film about the German present – a triumphant progress of the knowledge, the courage, the strength to fight and win for our German people.

A heroic film of facts – in the will of the Führer his people triumphs.

The Party-appointed chief press officer for the film, Herbert Seehofer, described the origins of the title in the *Licht-Bild-Bühne* for 23 October 1934:

The content of the film alone entirely justifies this title, since *Triumph of the Will* is by no means just a Party Rally film like last year's; it is intended as a much more true to life epic picture of the new Germany created by the victory of the movement as a triumph of the will on which it is based. The most significant stages of Germany's progress through twenty years of unprecedented destiny are to be re-created on film. These twenty years of dramatic events leading up to Nuremberg 1934 are to act as a prologue to the film, lasting a third of its entire length. 'This is how it was.' This theme determines the structure of the film, the framing action of which was scripted and shot by Walter Ruttmann . . .

In the same issue of the *Licht-Bild-Bühne* there is an account of additional material for *Triumph of the Will* which was not incorporated in the completed film. This material was evidently shot under the supervision of Leni Riefenstahl and Walter Ruttmann in the presence of Goebbels and a number of senior officials:

The scenes shot in the studio were reconstructed from earlier real events and situations. This was occasionally necessary, even when earlier original material existed, because since then production techniques have advanced at an unprecedented pace owing to the progress which has been achieved in the technical field, and the old material would have seemed dull in comparison. A number of situations, on the other hand, were reconstructed because they no longer apply. This was the case, for example, with the material on the Stock Exchange during inflation ...

On 1 May 1935, *Triumph of the Will* was awarded the National Film Prize. Goebbels commented on the choice:

The National Film Prize for 1934–35 has been awarded to Leni Riefenstahl for the Nuremberg Party Rally film *Triumph of the Will*.

This film marks a very fine achievement among the year's total production. It is topical, in that it shows the present; it conveys in monumental, hitherto unseen images the exhilarating events of our political life. It is a great cinematic vision of the Führer, here seen for the first time with a forcefulness which has not previously been revealed. This film has successfully avoided the danger of being merely a politically slanted film. It has translated the strong rhythm of these great times into convincing artistic terms; it is an epic, beating the tempo of marching formations, steel-like in its conviction, fired by a passionate artistry.

Here is Leni Riefenstahl herself on *Triumph of the Will*, in *Cahiers du Cinéma*, September 1965:

I showed what was happening then in front of our eyes, what everyone heard about. And the whole world was impressed by it ...

After the war *Triumph of the Will* brought me innumerable and severe difficulties. It was, certainly, a film commissioned by Hitler. But that was 1934, you must remember. And of course it was impossible for me, as a young woman, to foresee what was going to happen. In those days one believed in something beautiful. In reconstruction. In peace. The worst was still to come, but who knew that? Who talked about it? Where were the prophets? And how could I, of all people, have been one of them? How should I have known better than Winston Churchill, who even in 1935–36 was saying that he envied Germany its Führer? Could this be expected of me? Who could it be expected of? ...

I owe to this film, after my arrest by the French, several years in camps and prisons. But you will notice, if you see the film today, that it doesn't contain a single reconstructed scene. Everything in it is real. And there is no tendentious commentary for the simple reason that the film has no commentary at all. It is history. A purely historical film.

ii **Olympia**

In a statement issued in 1958, entitled 'The Production of the Olympia Films (Incorrect Statements and their Refutation)', Leni Riefenstahl herself commented on the background to her two films *Fest der Völker* (*Festival of Nations*) and *Fest der Schönheit* (*Festival of Beauty*):

1. . . . Among the duties of the Organisation Committee was the reporting of the Games in every form, which was not within the jurisdiction of the Propaganda Ministry. In this connection, Frau Leni Riefenstahl was commissioned to make the documentary film of the Games. The Propaganda Ministry had nothing to do with this decision, and furthermore its later protests were ignored.

And later in this submission:

2. It has been stated that the production of the Olympia film was supported and promoted by the Propaganda Ministry or by other National Socialist Party or State authorities. The truth is, however, that neither the Propaganda Ministry nor any other Party or State authority had any influence on the Olympic Games or on the production or format of the Olympia film, and that the Minister, Dr Goebbels, and his Ministry officials boycotted Leni Riefenstahl and the work on the Olympia film with every means at their disposal.

In the papers of the former Reich Ministry of Finance there is a 'Ministerial proposal', dated 15 October 1935, which states:

Ref. Request for new funds for publicity on 1936 Olympiad
   At the request of Minister Goebbels, Ministerial Secretary Ott referred to me the disposition of very considerable funds for:

1. Olympics publicity   300–350,000 RM
2. Olympia films   1·5 million RM

And as for paragraph 2.:

The Propaganda Ministry has submitted the draft contract for the production of an Olympics film, whereby Fräulein Leni Riefenstahl is assigned to produce a film on the Summer Olympics. The costs are estimated at 1·5 million RM.
   According to Ministerial Councillor Ott, Minister Goebbels wants the initial financing of the film to come from State funds.

Paragraph 1 of the contract assigns the production of the film to Leni Riefenstahl. In paragraph 2 the costs are estimated at 1·5 million Reichsmarks, and the payments are agreed on the following basis:

15 November 1935	300,000 RM
1 April 1936	700,000 RM
1 November 1936	200,000 RM
1 January 1937	300,000 RM

Leni Riefenstahl with Hitler and Goebbels at the premiere of *Olympia – Fest der Völker*

In addition there is an agreed remuneration of 250,000 RM for Leni Riefenstahl's services, inclusive of expenses ('travel, expenditure on cars'), and in paragraph 4 she agrees to 'render accounts on receipt of invoices in connection with the expenditure of the 1·5 million RM'.

In a letter of 18 December to the Reich Finance Minister, the Propaganda Minister states:

Subject to your agreement, therefore, I request for my projected budget for the financial year 1936 the required sum of 1·5 million RM. Since, however, there is a great deal of preliminary work on the film which must start immediately, for which a sum of 300,000 RM is required, I should be grateful if you will arrange to have this amount placed immediately at my disposal as an advance, and for my cash balance in January to be increased accordingly.

On 30 January 1936, the Propaganda Minister wrote to the district court at Charlottenburg, Berlin:

The Olympia-Film Co. Ltd. is being founded at the government's request and with government funds. In addition, the company's financial requirements for the production of the film are being met entirely from the state budget. The establishment of the company is urgent since the state is unwilling to appear publicly to be the producer of the film. It is proposed to liquidate the company after winding up the affairs relating to the production of the film.

The President of the State Film Department informed the district court on 12 February 1936:

It is thus not a matter of a private undertaking or an undertaking with ordinary film business objectives, but of a company which has been established simply for the purpose of the external organisation and production of the film in question. It is clearly impracticable to have the Treasury itself acting as film producer.

Leni Riefenstahl maintains that the Propaganda Ministry boycotted her work on the film and that:

Dr Goebbels ordered the Film Credit Bank, which came under the supervision of his Ministry, to block all further credits to the Olympia-Film Co. Ltd.

However, a 'report' of the 'preliminary examination by the Ministry of Popular Enlightenment and Propaganda', dated 16 October 1936, states that:

The actual amounts paid, however, on application from the company so far amount to the following:

3 February 1936	100,000 RM
5 May 1936	200,000 RM
15 July 1936	200,000 RM
1 August 1936	200,000 RM
11 August 1936	200,000 RM
16 September 1936	300,000 RM

Total 1,200,000 RM

To this was added on 15 October 1936 a further sum of 100,000 RM, so that by 1 November 1936, instead of the 700,000 RM provided by the contract, 1,300,000 RM will already have been paid.

The report states that the management of the funds provided by the government did not meet 'the requirements of proper business conduct' and were not in accordance with the principles of state budgetary regulations. Dr Goebbels appended comments to each page of the report. Nevertheless, he instructed his Ministerial Secretary Hanke 'not to deal with it ungenerously'. He increased the agreed funds of the Olympia-Film Co. Ltd. by 300,000 RM, the amount needed to complete the film. On 22 December 1936, Goebbels gave instructions that 'District Justice Pfennig of the State Film Department be placed at the disposal of the Olympia-Film Co. Ltd. as an adviser and be authorised to examine the random and business expenditure by this company.' The Minister requested his representative to 'report on his action within a given period'.

That Leni Riefenstahl's Olympia film production company was not a private concern but was under the jurisdiction of the government is revealed by a number of documents in the Federal Archives at Koblenz. A typical example is a letter from the company to the Ministry of Popular Enlightenment and Propaganda dated 10 October 1936. The Ministry is asked whether the company should participate in the Winter Charity.* 'On the one hand we do not consider it proper for us as a company to be excluded from this charity contribution; on the other hand, since, as you know, we are working with government funds, we do not wish to anticipate the Ministry's decision on the matter, and therefore leave it to their discretion.' The Ministry replied: 'Participation in the Winter Charity would involve expenditure of funds on a matter which lies outside your company's area of concern. I therefore request you to disregard any participation.'

In her 1958 document, Leni Riefenstahl maintains that she herself secured financial backing for the Olympics film by means of a distribution contract with Tobis-Filmkunst. But such a distribution contract could only be concluded with the Ministry's approval, and the government was supplied with information on all revenue. On 5 November 1938 the chief accountant responsible for controlling the expenditure of state funds asked the Propaganda Ministry 'at what point in time I am to consider the Olympia-Film Co. Ltd. dissolved, since the business of this company can to all intents and purposes be concluded'. Early in the war, on 17 May 1940, the Ministry could announce that 'the sums paid out of government funds, amounting altogether to 1,800,000 RM, are to be reimbursed'.

On 1 February 1943, the Ministry for Popular Enlightenment and Propaganda informed the Minister of Finance that 'the liquidation of the Olympia-Film Co. Ltd. has been concluded. According to the final statement of accounts to 31 December 1942, the net receipts so far obtained and discharged to the government amount to 114,066·45 RM. The Riefenstahl Film Co. Ltd. is authorised to supervise the further exploitation and management of the two Olympics films, and is to supply quarterly reports on the situation.'

* A compulsory tax, levied on postage stamps, etc., ostensibly for the relief of victims of winter.

iii **I Accuse**

The Jury Scene

Scene 133
Conference room

A bright, austere room. In the middle a long table with chairs. A cupboard. A water jug with glasses. Photograph of the Führer.

410–426

> *The jury and the three judges file through the door of the court. Tired from sitting for so long, they stretch themselves and walk about, forming small groups. In the course of the discussion some of them sit down, others support themselves on the backs of chairs, or casually rest a knee on the seat of a chair, inclining it towards them. Schoolmaster Schönbrunn, pharmacist Hummel and farmer Ziernicke are the first to enter.*

SCHOOLMASTER SCHÖNBRUNN (*taking off his glasses*): Now everything depends on Dr Lang.
HUMMEL: I wonder where he's got to.

> *The chairman, District Court President Griebelmeyer, followed by Assistant Judge Dr Scheu and Head Gamekeeper Rehefeld.*

REHEFELD: What if Dr Lang says that the Professor's wife wanted to die?
DR SCHEU: That would not be enough. He would have to say that she explicitly and seriously asked her husband to kill her.
REHEFELD: And then?
DR SCHEU: Then it is proved that this was a case of death by request, paragraph 216.
REHEFELD: And will he then be found guilty?
MAJOR DÖRING: But didn't the expert say that it can no longer be verified whether the poor woman died of her nervous troubles or whether he in fact killed her?
GRIEBELMEYER: Yes, if Dr Lang confirms that Frau Heyt would have died then in any case, we can acquit him, unless he has to be found guilty of attempted physical assault.
REHEFELD: Pity.
JUNIOR COUNSEL KNEWELS: Pity for the husband. But he shouldn't have done it under any circumstances.
HUMMEL: But the intention was good, to make the poor woman's end less painful.
SCHOOLMASTER SCHÖNBRUNN: Euthanasia, as the Latin scholars would say.

> *Knewels, Scheu and Griebelmeyer laugh.*

ROLFS: Eu – thana –

SCHOOLMASTER SCHÖNBRUNN: – sia – sia. From Thanatos, Greek for death . . . You see, gentlemen, the ancient Greeks and Romans allowed it.

DR SCHEU (*to Griebelmeyer*): I would never assume physical assault, because that certainly can't have been his intention.

KNEWELS (*to Scheu*): You would acquit him?

SCHEU: Yes, absolutely.

KNEWELS: Well, I'm not sure. The case has created such a fuss – other doctors might start killing their patients.

FARMER ZIERNICKE (*slowly*): That would be a great sin.

SCHOOLMASTER SCHÖNBRUNN: Gentlemen, if you ask me, Professor Heyt must be acquitted precisely because he is an example to all doctors. I know I'm raising a delicate point, but it's also a very rigid point in our moral and social values.

PHARMACIST HUMMEL: I don't know . . . If one simply allows this to happen . . . Do you think people would still go to the doctor?

SCHOOLMASTER SCHÖNBRUNN: Simply allow it to happen! We must . . .

LOCKSMITH ROLFS: Tell me, what happens if – and I've stuck my insurance stamps in all my life – if I fall ill one day? Would they simply kill me?

SCHOOLMASTER SCHÖNBRUNN: But, for heaven's sake! . . . The most important precondition is always the fact that the patient wants it.

ROLFS: But quite a few of us want it – for a moment.

HUMMEL: Yes, people who are mentally ill sometimes want it . . .

SCHOOLMASTER SCHÖNBRUNN: Yes, if a man is mad or depressive or otherwise incapable of making his own mind up, the state *must* take over the responsibility. Certainly, no doctor should be allowed to use his own discretion. We have to set up commissions of doctors and lawyers, genuine courts of law. But we can't go on watching thousands of people, who previously would have died quickly and peacefully, having to go on living for years in terrible pain simply because the doctors have learned how to prolong their miserable lives by artificial means.

FARMER ZIERNICKE (*slowly*): It is God's will. He sends us suffering so that people will follow the Cross and find eternal salvation.

MAJOR DÖRING: My dear Herr Ziernicke . . . With every respect for your Christianity – I'm not entirely free of it myself – but I just can't believe God is as cruel as that.

REHEFELD: Gentlemen, when we gamekeepers shoot an animal and it's still suffering, we put it out of its misery – and anyone who doesn't do that is a brute and no true huntsman.

ROLFS: But that's animals!

REHEFELD: Oh no, really! Sometimes man is no different from an animal who's been shot.

GRIEBELMEYER: Gentlemen, this discussion may be fascinating for a lawyer, but it isn't as simple as that.

If the Schoolmaster there is correct – that the right to kill should be taken from the individual and handed over to the state, which is anyway what happens in all questions of death – then there should of course be new laws for these . . . let's call them 'medical courts'.

SCHOOLMASTER SCHÖNBRUNN: The Romans had a law like that – but that was a heroic time, of course.

DR SCHEU: Five German states still had this law a hundred years ago.

MAJOR DÖRING: Which only goes to show that in many respects our ancestors were more rational than we are. Don't take it wrongly, gentlemen, but when hundreds of thousands of doctors, sisters and nurses are kept busy and huge buildings are equipped with laboratories and drugs and what have you, simply to keep alive a few miserable creatures who are either too mad to get anything out of life or dangerous criminals or really just like animals – and this at a time when we haven't enough people and rooms and money to keep the healthy in good health and look after mothers and their new-born children properly – well, that's really the most poppycock nonsense! The state simply has a duty to provide in the first place for those people who *are* after all the state – I mean those who work – and who as far as they're concerned are only too glad to die because they were once healthy and now can't bear it any longer – in my opinion, the state, which imposes a duty to die on us, must also concede us the right to die . . . I'm an old soldier and I know what I'm talking about.

SCHOOLMASTER SCHÖNBRUNN (*enthusiastically*): As the poet Lessing said, 'Should the freedom to die, which the gods have granted us for all the circumstances of life. – should one man be able to deny this to another?'

KNEWELS: Where did Lessing say that?

SCHOOLMASTER SCHÖNBRUNN: In 'Philotas'.

GRIEBELMEYER: Gentlemen, what old Lessing said in his poetic exuberance can't of course be applied to our laws which – for the moment at least – are different.

MAJOR DÖRING: As a jury we're naturally going to base our verdict on the law. But let me just say this – the laws are not there to stop people behaving reasonably and decently, and if they do they must be changed.

Close-up.

A COURT ATTENDANT *enters*: The witness Dr Lang is here, your honour.

GRIEBELMEYER: Well, come on then, gentlemen.

They all return slowly to the courtroom.

GRIEBELMEYER (*as he walks*): That was a really marvellous and refreshing mental exercise, gentlemen . . . We've seldom had such a stimulating jury, and also of course such an interesting case to discuss.

He disappears through the door.

ROLFS: Why did this witness Dr Lang turn up so late?

REHEFELD: If only he doesn't get the Professor into more trouble. That's what I'm really afraid of.

Security Service (SD) 'Reports from the Reich' on the public reaction to films

Public response to the film *I Accuse*

All the reports to hand indicate that the film *I Accuse* has aroused great interest in all areas of the Reich. In general it can be stated that with the help of extensive word-of-mouth publicity the film has been favourably received and discussed. Characteristic of the interest this film has provoked among the population is the fact that in many towns which had not yet seen it the film was being described – even by unsophisticated people – as one which simply had to be seen. The performances were generally enthusiastically received, and the film's content has actively stimulated people to think about it and has provoked lively discussion.

The film *I Accuse* raises two issues. Its main theme is the problem of *death on demand in cases of incurable illness*. A secondary theme deals with the question of putting an end to a life which is no longer worth living.

Judging by the reports received from all parts of the Reich, the majority of the German population accepts the film's proposition *in principle, though with some reservations* – that is, that people suffering from serious diseases for which there is no cure should be allowed a quick death sanctioned by law. This conclusion can also be applied to a number of religiously minded people.

The *attitude of the Church*, both Catholic and Protestant, is one of almost total rejection. There are reports that Catholic priests have used house visits to try to stop individual members of the population from going to see the film on the grounds that it is an inflammatory film directed against the Catholic Church or a state propaganda film designed to justify the killing of people suffering from hereditary illness.

In a number of cases the Catholic clergy has made only an indirect attack on the film, and according to reports has described it as being so good that it could be dangerous and 'as tempting as sin'. Despite this clear rejection of the film in Catholic circles, it has also been frequently reported that the film has in fact occasioned a conflict of opinion in the Catholic camp, with one faction supporting the principle that a person may be deprived of life if in particularly serious cases a panel of doctors has diagnosed an incurable illness and the administering of death could be considered a blessing for both parties. The other faction, however, still uses the word 'murder' in connection with the film.

All reports, even those coming from predominantly Catholic regions of the Reich, refer to the fact that the celebrated statements by Bishop Clemens August of Münster have in many cases been taken as a starting-point in discussions of the film, to the extent that there have been several comments about the film referring to it as an attempt to justify the state's measures now that the Bishop has attacked them.

For instance, the following comments have been heard:

'The film is quite interesting, but the story's just like the lunatic asylums where they're killing off all the crazy people now.'

'You can think what you like about all this, but who is going to guarantee that there won't be any abuses. As soon as laws like this are introduced it will be easy for the government to have anyone they consider undesirable declared incurable by a commission for any reason at all and then eliminate them. And moreover people with enough influence or money to criticise others will soon have somebody declared insane.'

In Protestant circles the open rejection of the film is not as strongly expressed. Yet here too people often say that life, which is God-given, can and should only be taken by God.

But we have also heard of *positive* opinions in Church circles. The Superintendent of Bautzen, for instance, said the following:

It will be the state's concern to prevent abuse, to take the responsibility and to ensure that loving kindness is extended to those incurables who are suffering. All this will be easier than the actual act of deliverance. As a Christian I must approve of this film.

As regards *medical circles*, a mostly positive response is reported to the questions raised by the film. Younger doctors in particular, apart from a few bound by religious beliefs, are completely in favour.

Doubts are expressed among older doctors particularly, despite their agreement in principle. In many cases doctors see it as a mistake to publicise the issues openly.

Here and there the question has been raised as to whether *medical diagnosis in borderline cases can really be sufficiently accurate to declare a patient incurable*.

For example, there are frequent cases of seriously ill patients who have been given up by all doctors and have then improved and lived on for years. Such cases are known to every doctor and every hospital. Other doctors mention that in their experience people, especially if they are seriously ill or old, talk only of their wish to die when they have temporarily succumbed to deep despair because of severe pain. However, in the moments when they have been free of pain these patients have shown remarkable spirit and have gone on hoping for recovery until the end.

Doubts have also been expressed about the film's suggestion of *medical committees*: each of the doctors serving on a committee would have to examine the patient independently. This would put an unnecessary emotional strain on the patient who, because of the repeated examinations, would become aware of what was intended.

Many doctors consider that the decision to intervene and help a patient could be left entirely to the German doctor's sense of responsibility. In practice, this kind of mercy killing already exists. Many doctors are taking it upon themselves, in cases where there is no prospect at all of recovery and the patient is suffering severe pain, to increase the dosage of the appropriate drug and so effect a painless death.

Indeed, the *legal profession* considers it a matter of urgency to provide medical practices of this kind with a basis in law. The legal difficulties which this would involve are considered to be great, since it would scarcely be possible to subject every relevant case of illness to legal examination, while on the other hand medical progress is such that an illness considered incurable today may be designated as curable tomorrow.

The *majority* of the German people has almost without exception reacted favourably to the issues raised, the following points, according to our reports, emerging as significant:

1. An essential precondition of the decision to declare a patient incurable is considered to be the convening of a *medical committee* in the presence of the family doctor.
2. Here and there the question has been raised as to whether mercy killing should be applied in all cases, since even patients with only a limited time to live are often still capable of doing productive work.
3. It is considered similarly essential where *euthanasia* is to be applied to obtain *the consent of the patient himself* or in the case of a feeble-minded mental patient *the permission of his relatives.*
4. In every case strict standards must be applied to prevent abuse; *in no case should the decision be left to an individual.*
5. In most people's opinion, *only the doctor* should be given the right, at his own discretion, to administer euthanasia.

On the whole the working classes are more favourably disposed to the change in the law suggested by the film than people from intellectual circles. The reason for this, according to our information, is that the socially less privileged classes are by nature more concerned about their own financial obligations. Most people respond to the film's immediate story, with the result that the theme of a long-suffering person being released from his misery is relegated to the background. Only doctors interpret the film in terms of this issue.

The negative attitudes towards the questions raised in the film are by far the minority opinion, and apart from the Church's point of view they can hardly be described as fundamentally contrary opinions.

To sum up, from the wealth of material to hand it emerges that in general the practice of euthanasia is approved, *when decided by a committee of several doctors with the agreement of the incurable patient and his relatives.*

The general approval finds its best expression in the words of the Major in the film:

'The state, which imposes a *duty* to die on us, must also concede us the *right* to die.'

From the Federal Archive, Koblenz
R 58/168, pp. 27–31, dated 15.1.1942

Letter from Wolfgang Liebeneiner dated 16 March 1965 (extract):

Munich, 16.3.65

Dear Minister,

You can imagine what it means to a citizen of good reputation to be accused by the highest representative of the law before the highest imaginable court of being an accessory to mass murder and to be counted among men whom one would never wish to meet. I have no doubt that you will provide the same court with a full indemnification as soon as you have informed yourself of the facts of the case.

The reason I am only writing to you today, after cabling you immediately after your speech, is that I have had some difficulty in obtaining an old document from Vienna which may perhaps provide you with a point of reference. This is a letter dated 14.2.1950, file number 14a Js 174/50, from Chief Prosecutor Kramer in Hamburg, who led the prosecution at the District Court. Enclosed were his negative findings concerning a suit filed against me for crimes against humanity in connection with the film *I Accuse.* This is the only suit filed against my film.

The film was shown, on application by the defence, at the 'Doctors' trial' before the Allied Military Tribunal at Nuremberg, but was rejected as evidence on the ground that it had 'nothing to do with the crimes on the indictment.' It was also shown, again on application by the defence, at last year's Limburg trial, where I was examined under oath. It was also seen by the Hamburg 'Culture Commission' in 1945. In *Der Spiegel* of 10.2.65, No. 7, I published a letter on the subject prompted by the announcement that a film on Nazi propaganda films was being made, to include *I Accuse*, which was no Nazi propaganda film but on the contrary a document of humanity in an inhuman time. It was mentioned in public for the fourth time in your speech.

I was no Party member; I was screened by British Field Security in Hamburg in the summer of 1945; I was the first case examined by the Hamburg Culture Commission in the autumn of 1945, and I was given permission to resume work. Minister Grimme, who knew of me through mutual friends, the Schulze-Boysens, who were executed in 1941, wanted me to take part in the setting up of the Göttinger film studios, which is why I appeared in 1946 at the British Assessment Centre in Bad Oeynhausen and later before the Hamburg 'Denazification Commission'. I have never been forbidden to work nor deprived of my liberty. In 1946, I directed the first production of Ida Ehre's *Draussen vor der Tür* for the Hamburg Kammerspiele; in 1948, I made the film *Liebe 47* [*Love 47*]; and among my later productions can be counted *1 April 2,000*, an Austrian government production (I am a German citizen), and the film *Das Tor zum Frieden* [*The Gate to Peace*], which I made for the Benedictine Order. In both cases my political past was again thoroughly investigated.

As far as I know, no one has ever brought a charge against me such as that filed in 1950 by a person unknown to me, and no one has lodged an accusation against me as you did last week. It is incomprehensible to me; since my film, for which I wrote both the final screenplay and the dialogue, dealt with death on demand. One of the three leading characters, the doctor played by Mathias Wieman, calls his colleague (Paul Hartmann), who he knows has killed his patient (Heidemarie Hatheyer) at her request, a murderer, and lodges a murder charge against him, only to withdraw the accusation later under the impact of another case from his own practice, thus agreeing with the then current criminal law (paragraph 216). The film's theme is death on demand, and all the arguments adduced for and against euthanasia relate to this.

The film's purpose was to test whether public opinion would approve of a law sanctioning death on demand within certain medical and legal safeguards. The test proved negative, the law was never passed, but the public debate on euthanasia which had been provoked immediately focused on the hitherto denied killing of mental patients and was instrumental in putting a stop to this. Above all this debate enabled Count Galen, for example, to preach from the pulpit against the euthanasia of mental patients. The word 'euthanasia' was thus introduced to people and naturally gave rise to some people's misconception that euthanasia meant the killing of mental patients and that therefore a 'euthanasia film' must be about this. Popular etymology, however, is no proof of the truth.

I made a film on this controversial subject to the best of my ability and with conviction. In 1932, I worked as an actor and production assistant under Rudolf Beer at the Deutsches Theater in Berlin on the production of *Engel unter uns* by Frantisek Langer, a Czech doctor and poet of the Jewish faith. In this play God sends an angel down to earth as a doctor in order to introduce death on demand – but the angel is put to death by Man. I had already come across the question in Maugham's *Sacred Flame* and I began to get interested in it, read Binding and Hoche's pamphlet, and was confronted by it again through several cases of serious war injuries; so I was not unprepared when in 1940 I was commissioned by Tobis to make a film on the subject. I have never dissociated myself from this work, though naturally I am aware of what a controversial issue it is and admit that it is a very vexed question as to whether it was right and sensible to make such a film during the Nazi period. Yet to this day I am convinced that the film has done good, perhaps even saved human lives, and naturally I can only expect to be attacked by those people who consider death on demand to be a crime under any circumstances. But of course I cannot allow it to be said in front of all the world that I am to be spoken of in the same breath as murderers, the kind of person one wouldn't wish to know . . .

Yours faithfully,
Wolfgang Liebeneiner

iv **Jud Süss**

Veit Harlan on *Jud Süss* in *Der Film*, 20 January 1940 (extract):

Naturally a film like this will encounter casting difficulties in Germany. The casting of the Jew Süss Oppenheimer himself is being negotiated at the moment. All the other Jewish parts in the film will be played by a single German character actor, an artist who has proved his unrivalled talent for characterisation on numerous occasions: Werner Krauss. Krauss will play the Super-Rabbi Loew, he will be the crooked little secretary Levi, and he will also make a brief appearance as another character. But it is by no means my intention here merely to draw attention to a bravura performance by a great actor; the casting, which incidentally was suggested by Krauss himself, has a much deeper significance. It is meant to show how all these different temperaments and characters – the pious Patriarch, the wily swindler, the penny-pinching merchant and so on – are ultimately derived from the same roots.

Around the middle of the film we show the Purim festival, a victory festival which the Jews celebrate as a festival of revenge on the Goyim, the Christians.

Here I am depicting original Jewry as it was then and as it even now continues unabated in what was Poland. (Harlan has just returned from a visit to Poland, where he made a study of the ghettos in a number of towns.) In contrast to this original Jewry we are presented with the Jew Süss, the elegant financial adviser to the Court, the clever politician, in short, the Jew in disguise . . .

Security Service (SD) 'Reports from the Reich' on the public reaction to films:

The current film programme

According to unanimous reports from all parts of the Reich, the film *Jud Süss* continues to receive an extraordinarily favourable response. The verdict on a film has rarely been as unanimous as it has been in the case of *Jud Süss*, which though unusually outspoken in its realistic treatment of offensive scenes is so artistically and so absolutely convincingly staged and with so much tension that 'one is totally gripped'. The total effect of the film can be gauged from such a spontaneous expression of opinion as 'One wants to go and wash one's hands'. Reports from Leipzig, Breslau, Oppeln, Salzburg, Potsdam, Reichenberg, Karlsruhe, Troppau, Dortmund, etc., suggest that the question of whether it would be a good thing for *children* to see the film is almost always answered in the negative by parents and teachers because of the film's extraordinarily powerful psychological after-effects.

Our reports are unanimous in suggesting that, in contrast to most other films showing at the moment, this film is commended and discussed above all for its *performances*; a report from Nuremberg, for instance, calls it 'frighteningly real' as far as the Jewish characters are concerned. In this respect, in fact, the film is much more impressive and convincing than *The Rothschilds* (Berlin). Among the scenes especially singled out by the public – apart from the rape scene – is the entry of the Jews and all their bags and baggage into Stuttgart. In fact this scene has repeatedly sparked off *demonstrations against the Jews* during the showing of the film. In Berlin, for example, people shouted, 'Ban the Jews from the Kurfürstendamm! Throw the last Jews out of Germany!'

The public's response to the character of the Duke of Württemberg was less unanimous. From comments received so far, the prevailing opinion is that the Duke is almost as despicable as the Jew Süss and that his death was a just punishment, which unfortunately came too early to enable him to learn the necessary attitude towards the Jew Süss and Jews in general.

From the Federal Archive, Koblenz
R 58/156, pp. 6–7, dated 28.11.1940

Report by Special Squad III/1 of the Strasburg Security Police:

Item: *Jud Süss*

An immensely impressive and effective film in direction, performances (of the mass scenes as well) and presentation of social history. Of primary interest is of course the 'Jewish question' as represented by the Jew Süss and the other members of his race, compared to which the absolutist regime with its debauchery and its extravagance recedes into the background. With its emphasis on cleverly chosen racial types (particularly effective in close-ups), its portrait of a religious scene completely alien to the German sensibility (Dance round the Golden Calf), apparently a record of an original ceremony shot in a Hungarian synagogue, and its dialogue, which pithily reflects the Jewish character, the film presents a once and for all picture of the 'Wandering Jew' and his parasitic existence as the essence of evil.

The film's effect is correspondingly powerful. The events on the screen are so realistic that audiences are constantly provoked to comment and shouting – an indication that the Party's educational work on the Jewish question is taking effect. 'Dirty pig Jew!', 'You Jewish swine!', 'Filthy Jewboy!' are comments often heard, particularly from women; and the rape scene, linked as it is with the only just bearable torture scene, really outrages people. While the expulsion of the Jews and the execution of Süss, when the full extent of his cowardice is revealed, is greeted with great satisfaction and relief ('Serves him right, dirty Jew', 'They should all be hanged!').

Heated discussion of the film continues outside on the street, and rarely has a film been talked about so much and so widely. The performances are almost always sold out, and there is only one verdict: *Jud Süss* is *the* best film in a long time.

A Correspondence

On 22 July 1948, before his trial in Hamburg, Veit Harlan wrote a letter to the American — formerly German — Rabbi Dr Prinz, the most significant passages of which are as follows:

Dear Rabbi Dr Prinz,

... In this trial I am least afraid for my own person. But however the trial goes, it is my deep conviction that it will bring misfortune, misfortune for Jewry, misfortune for the defeated German people, misfortune for the victorious Western Allies in their efforts to reconstruct the shattered foundations of a democracy which is to be based on the concept of human tolerance. The consequences of this trial will reach, via the press, the whole world. The same thing happened when I was acquitted by a Denazification committee after a seven months' hearing. This will be a sensational trial of the first order.

The film *Jud Süss* is on trial. The indictment states: an inflammatory film which slandered Jewry and therefore provoked the pogrom. The defence's answer will be: not an inflammatory film but a presentation of the Jewish question in artistic terms, not a distorted picture but an expression of important matters, of human concerns.

I will not talk in this letter of the pressures which were exerted on all artists. I would assure you, however, that I had nothing whatsoever to do with the Party, with anti-semitism, or with the whole National Socialist ideology.

It is a deplorable fact that in Germany a monstrous crime was perpetrated against Jewry. The Germans are therefore not entitled to talk about the all too human matter of the Jewish question, which is something only those who are free of any extensive guilt may do. If in spite of this understanding the defence is forced to do so, because to speak about it is required in the name of the law, the inevitable consequence will be to stir up the controversy again, when in the interests of peace it would be better to build a bridge between the two sides through an attitude of understanding and mutual tolerance ...

Yours respectfully,
Veit Harlan

Dr Prinz's answer, dated 24 July 1948:

Dear Mr Harlan,

Since my return from Germany I have given much thought both to your letter sent to me in Hamburg and to the matter of the film *Jud Süss*. I felt this to be my duty, since in Hamburg I realised what an important part the film, the trial and you yourself are playing in public opinion. In America I was not aware of the significance of this. The American press in general (with the exception of the German-speaking papers, which I read none too frequently) has devoted little attention to the matter. There were no big headlines and no sensational reports. The name Veit Harlan means nothing to the American public. I say this not to belittle your artistic ability and importance, but to give the whole matter a perspective which you – understandably – have lost.

In your letter you talk of big things, of 'misfortune for the victorious Western Allies', of 'misfortune for the German people', and even of 'misfortune for the Jewish people'. All this you see as the consequences of a trial which, in the name of justice and the law, is to decide how far you are to be answerable for the film *Jud Süss*, of which you say that it is not anti-semitic and that it has done little harm.

I am neither prosecutor nor judge. But I am a Jew and one who feels responsible for his people. Actors, directors, films and the whole of art are mere trivialities in the face of the death of many millions of people. They did not want to give up their lives. But we have lost our best people: artists, poets, scientists and simple, silent people who died the medieval death of torture. If only one of them suffered or was driven to his death because of your film, that would be reason enough to bring those people who placed their artistic gifts at the service of the executioners before the tribunal of the law.

That this has happened, moreover, not just once but in thousands of cases my inquiries here in London have established beyond a doubt. This is why your own person – as you say yourself – is unimportant. Why Veit Harlan – as a person, as an artist, as a man, should be more important than the many thousands of men, women and children who were dragged to their deaths by SS men who had been deeply impressed and deeply persuaded by your film – is beyond my comprehension. I have talked to people who saw with their own eyes, in Cracow in 1945 for instance, what effect your film had, and who later had to suffer for it themselves. Even perverted art can be perfect. And if – as I am told – your film is an artistic experience, then with all the resources of your great art it has succeeded in showing people through 'historical example' (what actual historical sources the film is based on is another question) that a Jew's sole desires are power, avarice, desecration and a deep-rooted meanness. And this at a moment when thousands of megaphones in Germany were broadcasting these very same things, and not for amusement but to pave the way for the greatest mass murder in human history. These facts – not your trial – were and are 'the misfortune of the defeated German people'. As for the misfortune the Jewish people may incur from the trial – let us worry about that. We have many worries. We can shoulder another one.

This letter is a serious attempt to say to you that it would be better for you, aware of your own guilt, to await the outcome of the trial with dignity and composure. The world's misfortune does not hang on your fate or on mine. The fortune and misfortune of all men depends on their own sacred will to do everything in their power to set up a new and more humane world which will oppose the human, moral and spiritual decline (which in Germany one sees and senses so strongly).

With all good wishes for this new world,

Yours,
Dr Joachim Prinz

II: Security Service (SD) Reports from the Reich on the public reaction to films

Audience response to the political instructional film *The Wandering Jew*

Following an extensive publicity campaign in the press and on radio, the documentary film *The Wandering Jew* has been *awaited with great interest by the public*, according to reports from all parts of the Reich. Numerous reports indicate that audiences are saying over and over again that the film's visual documentation, with its broad panorama of Jewish life and affairs, has completely lived up to these high expectations and that the film is more instructive, convincing and impressive than many an anti-Jewish tract. There has been unanimous acknowledgment of the high standards achieved in collating the available material into a single unit. Particularly favourable comment was made – as reported from Munich, Koblenz, Schwerin, Danzig, Halle, Königsberg, Potsdam and Berlin – on the way the *maps and statistics* catalogued the spread of Jewry (the comparison with rats is mentioned as particularly impressive) and its expanding influence on all areas of life and in all countries of the world. The shots of Jews in America have prompted particular comment. People were surprised by the open revelations of the Jewish influence in and dominance of the USA (Schwerin, Karlsbad). Particularly impressive were thought to be the scenes in which Jews were shown 'in their original state' and 'in European fashion' as men of the world (Leipzig), and in general the *juxtapositions* (Jewish ghetto – parade of German youth at the Party Rally) were thought to make an extraordinarily telling effect. According to a report from Munich, there was immediate relief and enthusiastic applause at the point in the film when the *Führer* appears and in his speech announces that a new war can only bring about the final annihilation of Jewry. Throughout the film the *sequences describing the history of the Rothschild family*, and in particular the information that members of the family had been naturalised in a number of different countries, thus establishing themselves as recognised citizens of the most important countries, were notably effective and convincing. These sequences and the contrasting of Jewish types from all parts of the world provided devastating proof – as can be deduced from numerous conversations – that for all his apparent adaptation to countries, languages and ways of life, a Jew is always a Jew.

Because of the very intensive publicity for the film and its impressive organisation of documentary evidence, the first performances produced remarkably high audience figures. But in some places audience interest has often soon fallen off, because the film has followed too quickly on the feature film *Jud Süss*. Since a large part of the population had already seen *Jud Süss*, it was very often assumed – according to the information to hand – that the documentary film *The Wandering Jew* had nothing really new to say. Reports received from, for example, Innsbruck, Dortmund, Aachen, Karlsruhe, Neustadt/Weinstrasse, Bielefeld, Frankfurt am Main and Munich all agree that it is often only the politically active sections of the population who have seen the documentary film while the typical film audience has largely avoided it, and that in some places there has been a word-of-mouth campaign against the film and its starkly realistic portrait of the Jews. The repulsive nature of the material and in particular the ritual slaughter scenes are repeatedly cited in conversation as the main reason for not seeing the film. The film is repeatedly described as an exceptional 'strain on the nerves' (Neustadt/ Weinstrasse). This is why attendance figures fell very sharply in places, particularly in North West, West and South Germany and in the Eastern region.* According to reports from West Germany and from Breslau, people have often been observed leaving the cinema in disgust in the middle of a performance. Statements like 'We've seen *Jud Süss* and we've had enough of Jewish filth' have been heard. There have been isolated cases of women and even younger men fainting during the ritual slaughter scenes. People have frequently claimed that *Jud Süss* had shown such a convincing picture of Jewry that this new and even more blatant evidence, following immediately after it in this documentary film, served no further purpose. On the other hand, numerous statements have been reported, particularly from the politically active sections of the population, expressing considerable appreciation of the film as a remarkably impressive document.

From the Federal Archive, Koblenz
R 58/157, pp. 7–9, dated 20.1.1941

Audience response to the film *Request Programme*

According to reports received to date from all parts of the Reich, the film *Request Programme* has had a *very sympathetic response* and has been enthusiastically *approved* by the public. Even before its release, extensive publicity had created great interest in the press, prompted by the popularity of request programmes in general. The continuing *record audience figures* provide convincing evidence that to make films on *subjects*, combined with the attempt to provide a fictional framework for *current events* which every cinemagoer knows from his own experience, is bound to ensure an above-average response from all sections of the population (Aachen, Kassel, Hannover, Kiel, Innsbruck, Weimar, Breslau, Karlsruhe, Griessen, Bielefeld, Bremen, Salzburg, Neustadt/Weinstrasse, Nuremberg, Oppeln, Frankfurt am Main, Schwerin, Neustettin). This attempt, and in particular the fact that

* i.e., Austria.

original material already known from the newsreels (the Olympic Games, Luftwaffe actions in the Polish campaign) was included in the film, is regarded as a novelty and distinctly enhances the liveliness and plausibility of the story. The frequently noted *word-of-mouth publicity for the film* centres particularly on references to the unusual *abundance of material on important events of recent years* (Olympic Games, Condor Legion in Spain, Polish campaign) and on the *frequent scenes of current actions in the war*. The film meets fully the general public's desire for *variety* and *topicality*. Especially popular are the *original scenes from a request programme*, some of which have been seen before in newsreels. There is a great deal of comment and discussion, according to the reports, about the fact that the infantry assault troops use a church, first as a landmark and a rendezvous and later as an observation post, which is at first completely undamaged and then becomes part of the battle zone (organ music) as it is bombarded and in the end destroyed. Moving though these scenes are, many people see them as contradicting the official German policy that churches should be kept out of the battle zone. On the other hand it is precisely these *church scenes* and the organ music which particularly appeal to those sections of the population who are still influenced by the Church (for example, Weimar, Kattowitz, Frankfurt am Main, Bielefeld, Paderborn). The overall quality of the *direction and the acting* was very highly regarded in many reports. Only the ending of the film has been criticised in various reports as a montage too geared to superficial effects.

> From the Federal Archive, Koblenz
> R 58/157, pp. 8–9, dated 17.2.1941

Audience response to the film *Ohm Krüger*

The reports from the various areas of the Reich all confirm that the general response to this film among all sections of the population has far exceeded the exceptionally high expectations aroused by a strong press campaign. The film is considered the *outstanding achievement of the current year in the cinema*, and particular mention is made of its superlative blending of political message, artistic construction and first-class performances. As a *popular success* it is in fact *exceptional*, as confirmed not only by the fact that every performance is sold out but also by the extensive word-of-mouth publicity and the frequent discussion about the film (*Hamburg, Koblenz, Berlin, Cologne, Leipzig, Munich*, Münster, Frankfurt am Main, etc.). Audiences are for the most part moved to silence while watching the film and are obviously deeply affected by it, and very unusually for a film this is still the case even after the performance. The fact that the film was completed in wartime is considered as distinctive evidence of the capacity of the German film industry.

There is no doubt that *in terms of propaganda the film completely fulfils its function as far as the general public is concerned*. The anti-British war mood has clearly significantly increased and consolidated, since in spite of considerable factual modifications the film is taken by large sections of the audience as a kind of historical document about a period of British colonial history. Younger viewers in particular seem to have received from the film their first clear picture of the defeat of the Boers (Oppeln). This impression is confirmed by a reportedly increased demand for literature about the Boers and their struggle for freedom. The film's description of British brutality has undoubtedly made a very strong impression, and the feeling is that psychologically the story has been constructed with a remarkable sense of the present mood of the German people towards England. Moreover the film has not been wasted on negative propaganda, but has brought out the moral and national values – though in really heroic fashion – of the Boer people's freedom struggle. The crowd scenes of the shooting of the Boer women are on all sides considered to be a particularly impressive highlight of the film. In the realism of this scene the film is thought to have reached the limits of what is tolerable.

In the main most audiences are so completely absorbed by the story that the outstanding achievements of both direction and performances are only later appreciated. The characterisation of Ohm Krüger is unanimously regarded as a really masterly piece of acting. On numerous occasions audiences from all sections of the population have expressed the view that the film provides the first convincing demonstration that it is cinematic artistry of the highest order which heightens a film's effectiveness as propaganda.

Critical opinions are in comparison numerically insignificant, and according to reports from various parts of the Reich they tend to raise the same fundamental questions. In the first place individual scenes are in some cases considered 'too heavily loaded' or too repugnant – for instance, the English missionaries' distribution of arms and prayer-books. The danger of such propaganda exaggerations is to reduce the plausibility of historical episodes in a film. According to the reports to hand, a number of spectators, particularly those with a knowledge of history but also the wider public, have raised the question of whether the in parts very strong propagandist and tendentious approach of the film was necessary at all, since in straightforward historical terms the suppression of the Boers is known to have been one of the most horrifying chapters of British brutality. The question was whether a greater historical authenticity might not have achieved the same or an even more convincing effect. It was frequently noted that after the performances audiences were reconsidering several of the calculated scenes, regarding them as historically inauthentic and so doubting the historical authenticity of more important parts of the story (*Hamburg, Koblenz, Münster, Düsseldorf, Danzig, Berlin, Munich, Kattowitz*). Knowledgeable audiences and people with experience of Africa have moreover raised the question of whether it was well-advised to make heroes of the Boers in this way, since along with their good features as a race they also display some very pronounced negative factors, and in terms of character, economics and politics they have by no means always played a positive role. The character of this mixed race is ambivalent, and in view of Greater Germany's colonial mission after the final victory they cannot be put forward as a Germanic ideal.

From the Federal Archive, Koblenz
R 58/160, pp. 13–15, dated 12.5.1941

Audience response to the film *The Great King*

Reports so far assembled from all parts of the Reich on the film *The Great King* all confirm the remarkable and sustained impression made by this work and its very favourable reception by the population, particularly among the general film-going public. Compared with the enthusiastic response which the film has had from nearly all sections of the population, critical opinions are in the minority. The wholly or partially negative views on the film are mostly found in the *Danube and Alpine regions*, where objections to the film's political and historical attitudes are based on a historical, pan-German point of view (Salzburg, Innsbruck, Klagenfurt, Troppau, Reichenberg, Karlsbad).

Criticism from these areas centres on the 'glorification of Prussianism' (Innsbruck). From a national perspective 'any particularised view, whether it comes from Vienna or as here from Berlin, is to be avoided' (Troppau). But even in these regions critical objections are in the minority compared with the favourable response from the bulk of film-goers. It has been noted in several places that the film is less appreciated by spectators with the least knowledge of history (Stettin, Cologne). Unsophisticated audiences 'couldn't follow the story' (Linz, Dresden, Stettin).

A number of reports state that *women* avoided the film because there was 'too much war in it' and because it was too much of a strain on the nerves (Dortmund, Aachen, Stuttgart, Stettin). In some places they 'started a veritable whispering campaign against it' (Karlsbad).

As to *the film's message*, opinion is divided. On the one hand the view is that the parallels between the Prussian situation of that time and the German situation of today are 'all too clumsily' drawn, even that the message is 'clumsily tacked on' (Berlin); and on the other hand reference is made to the film's early date and there is praise for the evident intention of sharpening the nation's endurance and will to win. The happy coincidence of the film's story and the everyday problems faced by the whole population has contributed to the film's unique success. For the first time a film has been concerned not simply to boost morale but to reach into people's hearts (Dresden).

Throughout the film audiences appear to have seen '*a mirror image of our own times*'. Many people have compared the King with the Führer, and while the film is running have recalled seeing a newsreel clip in which the Führer is seen alone at headquarters.

The performances are generally considered to be outstanding. Paul Wegener, as the Russian general whose good-natured appearance conceals an inner cunning, made a particularly strong impression. But some reports expressed doubts about the film's version of Chernikev, the Russian general. In reality, it is said, the general was 'an ardent admirer of Frederick' (Salzburg, Berlin, Cologne, Stettin). Otto Gebühr's performance as the King was almost unanimously well received. Gebühr is said to have played the part of his life.

The new image of the King which the film presents is the focal point of interest and in general the main topic of conversations about the film. Only isolated unsophisticated audiences have complained that they could not recognise 'their old Fritz' (Stettin). But in the public at large the new image of Frederick has proved to be enormously impressive and absorbing. It was precisely this which made the film such an unusual experience (Munich). It stripped the legendary mask from Frederick's genius and painted a candid portrait of·the King in all his austerity and human greatness. Little remained of the silent cinema's resplendent 'Fridericus' and nothing of the father-figure to soldiers and country image of popular legend. So, in spite of all the criticism, the film had managed to remove the romantic smokescreen, the patriotic pathos and the bourgeois morality from Prussian history and to give our people some idea of the lonely, glacial atmosphere surrounding a head of state responsible for a nation's destiny (Munich).

The ending of the film provoked some isolated criticism. People felt that the photographic montage could have been dispensed with. The 'eye of Frederick' suggested an unfortunate association with the 'eye of God' (Nuremberg, Reichenberg). On the other hand, some people thought that this very final scene with the 'eye of the King' worked marvellously in film terms (Berlin). In addition, there have been frequent comments to the effect that a film which was meant to show the people the King as he really was ought to have given more emphasis to Frederick's achievements in peacetime, his colonising activities and his spiritual work. The story was too exclusively concerned with war.

On the whole those audiences who rated the Bismarck film as so far unsurpassed in its representation of a historical subject placed this film second. Others consider *The Great King* 'the best film ever to have reached the screen' (Nuremberg). Next to the films which were awarded the 'Film of the Nation' category, this was the most important work of cinema from an educational and artistic point of view (Stuttgart).

From the Federal Archive, Koblenz
R 58/172, pp. 12–14, dated 28.5.1942

Bibliography

Books

Adler, H. G. *Die verheimlichte Wahrheit. Theresienstädter Dokumente.* Tübingen, 1958.

Albrecht, Gerd *Nationalsozialistische Filmpolitik.* Stuttgart, Ferdinand Enke Verlag, 1969.

Almanach der Deutschen Filmschaffenden 1943. Berlin, Max Hesses Verlag, 1943.

Bauer, Alfred *Deutscher Spielfilmalmanach 1929–1950.* Berlin, Filmblätter Verlag, 1950.

Barning, Cornelia *Vom 'Abstammungsnachweis' zum 'Zuchtwart'. Vokabular des Nationalsozialismus.* Berlin, 1964

Belling, Curt *Der Film im Dienste der Partei.* Berlin, Lichtspielbühne, 1937.

Boberach, Heinz *Meldungen aus dem Reich.* Neuwied, 1965.

Boelcke, Willi A. *Secret Conferences of Dr. Goebbels: The Nazi Propaganda War, 1939–1945.* New York, Dutton, 1970.

Bramsted, Ernest K. *Goebbels and National Socialist Propaganda 1925–1945.* Ann Arbor, Michigan State University Press, 1965.

Brenner, Hildegard *Die Kunstpolitik des Nationalsozialismus.* Hamburg, Rowohlt, 1963.

Bucher, Felix *Germany* (Screen Series). London, A. Zwemmer Limited, 1970.

Bullock, Alan *Hitler, a Study in Tyranny.* London, Penguin, 1969.

Control Commission for Germany, Information Services Commission *Catalogue of*

Forbidden German Features and Short Film Productions Held in Zonal Film Archives of the Film Section, Information Services Division. Hamburg, 1951.

Courtade, Francis, and Cadars, Pierre *Histoire du Cinéma nazi.* Paris, Eric Losfeld, 1972.

Der Deutsche Film. Berlin, Reichsfilmkammer, 1941.

Domarus, Max *Hitler. Reden und Proklamationen 1932–1945.* Munich, 1965.

Erikson, Erik H. *Childhood and Society.* New York, W. W. Norton, 1963.

Giese, Hans-Joachim *Die Film-Wochenschau im Dienste der Politik.* Dresden, 1940.

Gilbert, G. M. *Nuremberg Diary.* New York, New American Library, 1971.

Goebbels, Joseph *Goebbels: Diaries 1942–1943.* Ed. Louis Lochner. Westport, Greenwood, 1941.

—— *Das eherne Herz.* Reden und Aufsätze aus den Jahren 1941–1942. Munich, Zentralverlag der N.S.D.A.P., 1943.

Günter, Walther *Der Film als politisches Führungsmittel.* Leipzig, Robert Noske, 1934.

Harlan, Veit *Im Schatten meiner Filme.* Gütersloh, Sigbert Mohn Verlag, 1966.

Heiber, Helmut *Joseph Goebbels.* Berlin, 1962.

Heyde, Ludwig *Presse, Rundfunk und Film im Dienste der Volksführung.* Dresden, Verlag M. Dittert, 1943

Hippler, Fritz *Betrachtungen zum Filmschaffen.* Berlin, Max Hesses Verlag, 1942.

Hitler, Adolf *Mein Kampf.* Trans. R. Mannheim. London, Hutchinson, 1969.

Hofer, Walther *Der Nationalsozialismus. Dokumente 1933–1945.* Frankfurt, 1957.

Hull, David Stewart *Film in the Third Reich.* Berkeley, University of California Press, 1969.

Jacobsen, H. A. *1939–1945. Der zweite Weltkrieg in Chronik und Documenten.* Darmstadt, 1961.

Jahrbuch der Reichsfilmkammer 1937. Berlin, Max Hesses Verlag, 1937.

Jahrbuch der Reichsfilmkammer 1938. Berlin, Max Hesses Verlag, 1938.

Jahrbuch der Reichsfilmkammer 1939. Berlin, Max Hesses Verlag, 1939.

Jason, A. *Das Filmschaffen in Deutschland 1935 bis 1939.* Berlin, Institut für Konjunkturgorschung, 1940.

—— *Das Filmschaffen in Deutschland 1940–1941.*

—— *Das Filmschaffen in Deutschland 1942–1943.*

Kalbus, Oskar *Vom Werden deutscher Filmkunst.* II Teil: Der Tonfilm. Altona-Bahrenfeld, 1935.

Kardorff, Ursula von *Diary of a Nightmare.* Trans. E. Butler. London, Hart-Davis, 1965.

Kliesch, Hans-Joachim *Die Film- und Theaterkritik im NS-Staat.* Berlin, 1957.

Klimsch, G. W. *Die Entwicklung des nationalsozialistischen Filmmonopols von 1930 bis 1940, in vergleichender Betrachtung zur Pressekonzentration.* University of Munich, 1954 (unpublished thesis).

Koch, Heinrich, and Braune, Heinrich *Von Deutscher Filmkunst.* Berlin, Verlag Hermann Scherping, 1943.

Kockenrath, Hans-Peter *Der Film in Dritten Reich. Dokumentation.* University of Cologne, 1963 (unpublished).

Kolb, Richard, and Siekmeier, Heinrich *Rundfunk und Film im Dienste nationaler Kultur*. Düsseldorf, Friedrich Floeder Verlag, 1933.

Kracauer, Siegfried *From Caligari to Hitler*. Princeton, Princeton University Press, 1947.

Kriegk, Otto *Der Deutsche Film im Spiegel der Ufa*. Berlin, UFA-Buchverlag, 1943.

Leiser, Erwin '*Mein Kampf*'. (Film script, 1960.) In *Filme contra Faschismus*. Berlin, 1965.

——— *Eichmann und das Dritte Reich*. Film script. Zürich, 1961 (unpublished).

Manvell, Roger, and Fraenkel, Heinrich *Dr Goebbels*, London, Heinemann, 1960.

Mead, Margaret, and Métraux, Rhoda *The Study of Culture at a Distance*. Chicago, 1953.

Mitscherlich, Alexander and Margaret *Die Unfähigkeit zu trauern*. Munich, 1967.

Mitscherlich, Alexander, and Mielke, Fred *Medizin ohne Menschlichkeit. Dokumente der Nürnberger Ärzteprozesse*. Heidelberg, 1949.

Mosse, George L. *Nazi Culture*. New York, Grossett and Dunlap, 1966.

Neumann, Carl, Belling, Curt, and Betz, Hans-Walther *Film 'Kunst', Film-Kohn, Film-Korruption*. Berlin, Verlag Hermann Scherping, 1937.

Oley, Hans, and Hellwig, Joachim . . . *wie einst Lili Marleen*. Berlin, Verlag der Nation (n.d.).

Picker, Henry *Hitlers Tischgespräche im Führerhauptquartier* 1941–1942. Bonn, 1951.

Prado, Herbert, and Schiffner, Siegfried *Jud Süss. Historisches und juristisches Material zum Fall Veit Harlan*. Hamburg, Auerdruck, 1949.

Propaganda und Gegenpropaganda in Film 1933–45. Vienna, Oesterreichisches Filmmuseum, 1972.

Rabenalt, Arthur Maria *Film im Zwielicht*. Munich, Copress Verlag, 1958.

Rathgeb, Kaspar *Die Filmindustrie als Problem der Handelspolitik*. Birkeneck, Druckerei St Georgsheim, 1935.

Rauschning, Hermann *Gespräche mit Hitler*. Zürich, 1940.

Reitlinger, Gerald *The Final Solution*. New York, Barnes, 1961.

Riefenstahl, Leni *Hinter den Kulissen des Reichsparteitagfilms*. Munich, Zentralverlag der N.S.D.A.P., Franz Eher Nachf., 1935.

Riess, Curt *Das gab's nur einmal*. Hamburg, Verlag der Sternbücher, 1956.

Ruehl, Raimond *Kolberg. Der letzte 'Film der Nation'* (unpublished).

Sander, Agnes-Ulrike *Jugend und Film*. Zentralverlag der N.S.D.A.P., Franz Eher Nachf., 1944.

Schenzinger, Karl Aloys *Der Hitlerjunge Quex*. Berlin, 1932.

Schneider, Wolf *Das Buch vom Soldaten*. Düsseldorf, 1964.

Seraphim, Hans Günther *Das politische Tagebuch Alfred Rosenbergs*. Munich, 1956.

Traub, Hans *Der Film als politisches Machtmittel*. Munich, München Druck- und Verlagshaus, 1933.

——— *Die Ufa*. Berlin, Ufa-Buchverlag, 1943.

Wolf, Kurt *Entwicklung und Neugestaltung der deutschen Filmwirtschaft seit 1933*. Heidelberg, Druckerei Hermann Meister, 1938.

Wollenberg, H. H. *Fifty Years of German Film*. London, Falcon Press, 1948.

Wulf, Joseph *Aus dem Lexicon der Mörder*. Gütersloh, Sigbert Mohn Verlag, 1963.
—— *Die Bildenden Künste im Dritten Reich*. Gütersloh, Sigbert Mohn Verlag, 1963.
—— *Theater und Film im Dritten Reich*. Gütersloh, Sigbert Mohn Verlag, 1964.
Zeman, Z. A. B. *Nazi Propaganda*. Oxford, Oxford University Press, 1964.

Articles

Albrecht, Gerd *Korrektur zum Nazifilm*. In *Film* (W. Germany), October 1963.
Altmann, John *Movies' Role in Hitler's Conquest of German Youth*. In *Hollywood Quarterly* (Berkeley), Vol. III, No. 4.
Bateson, Gregory *Cultural and Thematic Analysis of Fictional Films*. In *Transactions of the New York Academy of Sciences*, Series II, Vol. 5, No. 4, February 1943.
Blobner, Helmut, and Holba, Herbert *Jackboot Cinema*. In *Films and Filming* (London), December 1962.
Delahaye, Michel *Leni et le loup: entretien avec Leni Riefenstahl*. In *Cahiers du Cinéma* (Paris), September 1965 (translated in *Cahiers du Cinéma in English*).
Fischer, Heinrich *The Theatre and Film in Nazi Germany*. In *Tricolor* (New York), July–August 1945.
Film Culture, No. 56–57, Spring 1973. Several articles on and interview with Leni Riefenstahl.
Gregor, Ulrich *A Comeback for Leni Riefenstahl?*. In *Film Comment* (New York), Winter 1965.
Hitchens, Gordon *An Interview with a Legend*. In *Film Comment* (New York), Winter 1965.
Leiser, Erwin *La vérité sur Leni Riefenstahl et Le Triomphe de la volonté*. In *Cinéma 69*, No. 133, February 1969.
Marcorelles, Louis *The Nazi Cinema*. In *Sight and Sound* (London), Autumn 1955.
Phillips, M.S. *The Nazi Control of the German Film Industry*. In *Journal of European Studies*, 1, 1971.
Regel, Helmut *Zur Topographie des NS-Films*. In *Filmkritik* (Frankfurt), January 1966.

Select Filmography

The following abbreviations are used: *Dir* (Director), *Sc* (Screenplay), *L.P.* (Leading Players).

(N.B. For a complete list of films produced during the Third Reich see Dr Alfred Bauer's *Deutscher Spielfilmalmanach 1929–1950*)

Der alte und der junge König (1935) (pp. 50, 113).
Dir: Hans Steinhoff. *Sc:* Thea von Harbou, Rolf Lauckner. *L.P.:* Emil Jannings, Werner Hinz, Claus Clausen.

Andreas Schluter (1942) (p. 109)
Dir: Herbert Maisch. *Sc:* Helmut Brandis, Herbert Maisch. From the novel *Der Münzturm* by Alfons von Czibulka. *L.P.:* Heinrich George, Theodor Loos, Mila Kopp.

Annelie (1941) (pp. 62–63)
Dir: Josef von Baky. *Sc:* Thea von Harbou, from the play by Walter Lieck. *L.P.:* Luise Ullrich, Werner Krauss, Karl Ludwig Diehl.

Anschlag auf Baku (1942) (p. 103)
Dir: Fritz Kirchhoff. *Sc:* Hand Weidemann, Hans Wolfgang Hillers. *L.P.:* Willy Fritsch, Renė Deltgen, Lotte Koch.

Auf Wiedersehen, Franziska (1941) (p. 65)
Dir: Helmut Käutner. *Sc:* Helmut Käutner, Curt Johannes Braun. *L.P.:* Marianne Hoppe, Hans Söhnker, Hermann Speelmans.

Befreite Hände (1939) (p. 13)
Dir: Hans Schweikart. *Sc:* Erich Ebermayer, Kurt Heuser, from the novel by Erich Ebermayer. *L.P.:* Brigitte Horney, Olga Tschechowa, Ewald Balser.

Besatzung Dora (1943) (pp. 63, 65)
Dir: Karl Ritter. *Sc:* Fred Hildenbrand, Karl Ritter. *L.P.:* Hannes Stelzer, Carsta Löck, Hubert Kiurina.

Bismarck (1940) (pp. 43, 50, 75, 106–107, 111, 118–119)
Dir: Wolfgang Liebeneiner. *Sc:* Rolf Lauckner, Wolfgang Liebeneiner. *L.P.:* Paul Hartmann, Friedrich Kayssler, Werner Hinz.

Carl Peters (1941) (pp. 50, 75, 99, 103–105, 107)
Dir: Herbert Selpin. *Sc:* Ernst von Salomon, Walter Zerlett-Olfenius, Herbert Selpin. *L.P.:* Hans Albers, Karl Dannemann, Fritz Odemar.

Der Choral von Leuthen (1933) (pp. 112–113)
Dir: Carl Froelich. *Sc:* Johannes Brandt, Ilse Spath-Baron, from an idea by Friedrich Pflughaupt suggested by the novel *Fridericus* by Walter von Molo. *L.P.:* Otto Gebühr, Olga Tschechowa, Elga Brink.

D III 88 (1939) (pp. 51–52)
Dir: Herbert Maisch. *Sc:* Hans Bertram, Wolf Neumeister. *L.P.:* Christian Kayssler, Otto Wernicke, Heinz Welzel.

Die Entlassung (1942) (pp. 62, 112, 119–120)
Dir: Wolfgang Liebeneiner. *Sc:* Curt Johannes Braun, Felix von Eckardt. *L.P.:* Emil Jannings, Werner Krauss, Werner Hinz.

Der ewige Jude (1940) (pp. 75, 76, 78, 85–88, 157–158)
Dir: Fritz Hippler. *Sc:* Eberhard Taubert.

Fahrt ins Leben (1940) (p. 21)
Dir: Bernd Hofmann. *Sc:* Bernd Hofmann. *L.P.:* Ruth Hellberg, Hedwig Bleibtreu, Herbert Hübner.

Feinde (1940) (p. 69)
Dir: Viktor Tourjansky. *Sc:* Emil Burri, Arthur Luethy, Viktor Tourjansky. *L.P.:* Brigitte Horney, Willy Birgel, Iwan Petrovich.

Das Flötenkonzert von Sanssouci (1930) (p. 21)
Dir: Gustav Ucicky. *Sc:* Walter Reisch. *L.P.:* Otto Gebühr, Renate Müller, Hans Rehmann.

Flüchtlinge (1933) (pp. 22, 29–30, 53, 101)
Dir: Gustav Ucicky. *Sc:* Gerhard Menzel, from his own novel. *L.P.:* Hans Albers, Käthe von Nagy, Eugen Klopfer.

Frauen sind doch bessere Diplomaten (1941) (p. 62)
Dir: Georg Jacoby. *Sc:* K. G. Külb, Gustav Kampendonk. *L.P.:* Marika Rökk, Willy Fritsch, Aribert Wäscher.

Fridericus (1936) (p. 113)
Dir: Johannes Meyer. *Sc:* Erich Kröhnke, Walter von Molo, from the novel by Walter von Molo. *L.P.:* Otto Gebühr, Hilde Körber, Lil Dagover.

Friedrich Schiller (1940) (pp. 107–109)
Dir: Herbert Maisch. *Sc:* Walter Wassermann, C. H. Diller, from an idea by Paul Josef Cremers. *L.P.:* Horst Caspar, Heinrich George, Lil Dagover.

Friesennot (1935) (pp. 40–42)
Dir: Peter Hagen. *Sc:* Werner Kortwich. *L.P.:* Friedrich Kayssler, Inkijinoff, Helene Fehdmer.

Der Fuchs von Glenarvon (1940) (pp. 13, 97)
Dir: Max W. Kimmich. *Sc:* Wolf Neumeister, Hans Bertram, from the novel by Nicola Rohn. *L.P.:* Olga Tschechowa, Karl Ludwig Diehl, Ferdinand Marian.

Germanin (1943) (p. 103)
Dir: Max W. Kimmich. *Sc:* Max W. Kimmich, Hans Wolfgang Hillers, from the novel by Hellmuth Unger. *L.P.:* Peter Petersen, Lotte Koch, Luis Trenker.

Gold (1934) (p. 19)
Dir: Karl Hartl. *Sc:* Rolf E. Vanloo. *L.P.:* Hans Albers, Brigitte Helm, Michael Bohnen.

GPU (1942) (pp. 44–45)
Dir: Karl Ritter. *Sc:* Andrews Engelman, Felix Lützkendorf, Karl Ritter, from an idea by Andrews Engelman. *L.P.:* Laura Solari, Will Quadflieg, Andrews Engelman.

Grosse Freiheit Nr. 7 (1944) (p. 15)
Dir: Helmut Käutner. *Sc:* Helmut Käutner, Richard Nicolas. *L.P.:* Hans Albers, Ilse Werner, Hans Söhnker.

Der grosse König (1942) (pp. 62, 112, 113–118, 121, 161–163)
Dir: Veit Harlan. *Sc:* Veit Harlan. *L.P.:* Otto Gebühr, Kristina Söderbaum, Gustav Fröhlich.

Die grosse Liebe (1942) (pp. 61, 63–65)
Dir: Rolf Hansen. *Sc:* Peter Groll, Rolf Hansen, from an idea by Alexander Lernet-Holenia. *L.P.:* Zarah Leander, Viktor Staal, Paul Hörbiger.

Hans Westmar (1933) (pp. 24, 35–36, 38–39)
Dir: Franz Wenzler. *Sc:* Hanns Heinz Ewers, from his own book *Horst Wessel*. *L.P.:* Emil Lohkamp, Paul Wegener, Carla Bartheel.

Heimkehr (1941) (pp. 62, 68–72, 76)
Dir: Gustav Ucicky. *Sc:* Gerhard Menzel. *L.P.:* Paula Wessely, Peter Petersen, Attila Hörbiger.

Heldentum und Todeskampf unserer Emden (1934) (p. 57)
Dir: Louis Ralph. *Sc:* Louis Ralph. *L.P.:* Louis Ralph, Willi Kaiser-Heyl, Fritz Greiner.

Henker, Frauen und Soldaten (1935) (p. 95)
Dir: Johannes Meyer. *Sc:* Max W. Kimmich, Jacob Geis, from the novel *Ein*

Mannsbild namens Prack by Fritz Reck-Malleczewen. *L.P.:* Hans Albers, Charlotte Susa, Jack Trevor.

Der Herrscher (1937) (pp. 49–50)
Dir: Veit Harlan. *Sc:* Thea von Harbou, Curt Johannes Braun, from the play *Vor Sonnenuntergang* by Gerhart Hauptmann. *L.P.:* Emil Jannings, Marianne Hoppe, Maria Koppenhöfer.

Himmelhunde (1941) (pp. 33, 65)
Dir: Roger von Norman. *Sc:* Philipp Lothar Mayring, from an idea by Hanns Fischer-Gerhold and Hans Heise. *L.P.:* Malte Jäger, Waldemar Leitgeb, Lutz Götz.

Hitlerjunge Quex (1933) (pp. 24, 35–39)
Dir: Hans Steinhoff. *Sc:* Karl Aloys Schenzinger, Bobby E. Lüthge, from the novel by Karl Aloys Schenzinger. *L.P.:* Heinrich George, Berta Drews, Claus Clausen.

Hochzeit auf Bärenhof (1942) (p. 63)
Dir: Carl Froelich. *Sc:* Jochen Kuhlmey, Gustav Lohse, from the novella *Jolanthes Hochzeit* by Hermann Sudermann. *L.P.:* Heinrich George, Paul Wegener, Ilse Werner.

Der höhere Befehl (1935) (p. 96)
Dir: Gerhard Lamprecht. *Sc:* Philipp Lothar Mayring, Kurt Kluge, Karl Lerbs. *L.P.:* Lil Dagover, Karl Ludwig Diehl, Heli Finkenzeller.

Hundert Tage (1935) (pp. 53–55)
Dir: Franz Wenzler. *Sc:* Karl Vollmöller, Franz Wenzler, from the play by Benito Mussolini and Giovacchino Forzano. *L.P.:* Werner Krauss, Gustaf Gründgens, Kurt Junker.

Ich klage an (1941) (pp. 24, 62, 89–94, 143–151)
Dir: Wolfgang Liebeneiner. *Sc:* Eberhard Frowein, Harald Bratt, from the novel *Sendung und Gewissen* by Hellmuth Unger and an idea by Harald Bratt. *L.P.:* Heidemarie Hatheyer, Paul Hartmann, Mathias Wieman.

Ihr erstes Erlebnis (1939) (p. 13)
Dir: Josef von Baky. *Sc:* Juliane Kay, from the novel *Tochter aus gutem Hause* by Susanne Kerckhoff. *L.P.:* Ilse Werner, Johannes Riemann, Volker von Collande.

Jud Süss (1940) (pp. 62, 76, 78, 80–85, 132, 152–156)
Dir: Veit Harlan. *Sc:* Ludwig Metzger, Eberhard Wolfgang Möller, Veit Harlan. *L.P.:* Ferdinand Marian, Werner Krauss, Heinrich George.

Junge Adler (1944) (pp. 65–66)
Dir: Alfred Weidenmann. *Sc:* Herbert Reinecker, Alfred Weidenmann, from an idea by Herbert Reinecker. *L.P.:* Willy Fritsch, Herbert Hübner, Dietmar Schönherr.

Kadetten (1941) (pp. 44–116)
Dir: Karl Ritter. *Sc:* Felix Lützkendorf, Karl Ritter, from an idea by Alfons Menne. *L.P.:* Mathias Wieman, Andrews Engelman, Carsta Löck.

Kameraden auf See (1938) (p. 42)
Dir: Heinz Paul. *Sc:* Peter Francke, J. A. Zerbe, from an idea by Toni Huppertz and J. A. Zerbe. *L.P.:* Paul Wagner, Fred Döderlein, Rolf Weih.

Kampfgeschwader Lützow (1941) (p. 32)
Dir: Hans Bertram. *Sc:* Hans Bertram, Wolf Neumeister, Heinz Orlovius. *L.P.:* Christian Kayssler, Hermann Braun, Heinz Welzel.

Kitty und die Weltkonferenz (1939) (p. 96)
Dir: Helmut Käutner. *Sc:* Helmut Käutner, from the play *Weltkonferenz* by Stefan Donat. *L.P.:* Hannelore Schroth, Paul Hörbiger, Fritz Odemar.

Kolberg (1945) (pp. 122–133)
Dir: Veit Harlan. *Sc:* Veit Harlan, Alfred Braun. *L.P.:* Heinrich George, Kristina Söderbaum, Horst Caspar.

Kopf hoch, Johannes! (1941) (p. 65)
Dir: Victor de Kowa. *Sc:* Toni Huppertz, Wilhelm Krug, Felix von Eckhardt, from an idea by Toni Huppertz. *L.P.:* Albrecht Schoenhals, Dorothea Wieck, Klaus Detlef Sierck.

Legion Condor (1939) (p. 43)
Dir: Karl Ritter (supervised by Air Force General Wilberg). *Sc:* Felix Lützkendorf, Karl Ritter. *L.P.:* Paul Hartmann, Albert Hehn, Heinz Welzel.

Leinen aus Irland (1939) (pp. 75, 76–77)
Dir: Heinz Helbig. *Sc:* Harald Bratt, from the play by Stefan von Kamare. *L.P.:* Irene von Meyendorff, Rolf Wanka, Siegfried Breuer.

Das Lied der Wüste (1939) (p. 13)
Dir: Paul Martin. *Sc:* Walther von Hollander, Paul Martin, from a report by Werner Illing. *L.P.:* Zarah Leander, Herbert Wilk, Gustav Knuth.

Ein Mann will nach Deutschland (1934) (p. 95)
Dir: Paul Wegener. *Sc:* Philipp Lothar Mayring, Fred Andreas, from the novel by Fred Andreas. *L.P.:* Karl Ludwig Diehl, Brigitte Horney, Siegfried Schürenberg.

Der Marsch zum Führer (1940) (p. 12)
Dir/Sc: not credited. Hitler Youth film.

Mein Leben für Irland (1941) (pp. 97–99)
Dir: Max W. Kimmich. *Sc:* Toni Huppertz, Max W. Kimmich. *L.P.:* Anna Dammann, Werner Hinz, René Deltgen.

Mein Sohn, der Herr Minister (1937) (pp. 42, 50–51)
Dir: Veit Harlan. *Sc:* H. G. Külb, Edgar Kahn, from the play *Fiston* by André Birabeau. *L.P.:* Hans Moser, Paul Dahlke, Hans Brausewetter.

Morgenrot (1933) (pp. 20–22)
Dir: Gustav Ucicky. *Sc:* Gerhard Menzel, from an idea by R. Freiherr von Spiegel. *L.P.:* Rudolf Forster, Adele Sandrock, Fritz Genschow.

Nanette (1939) (p. 13)
Dir: Erich Engel. *Sc:* Jochen Huth. *L.P.:* Jenny Jugo, Hans Söhnker, Albrecht Schoenhals.

Nora (1944) (p. 16)
Dir: Harald Braun. *Sc:* Jacob Geis, Harald Braun, from the play *A Doll's House* by Henrik Ibsen. *L.P.:* Luise Ullrich, Viktor Staal, Gustav Diessl.

Ohm Krüger (1941) (pp. 62, 99–103, 107, 132, 159–161)
Dir: Hans Steinhoff, with Herbert Maisch and Karl Anton. *Sc:* Harald Bratt, Kurt Heuser, from themes suggested by the novel *Mann ohne Volk* by Arnold Krieger. *L.P.:* Emil Jannings, Lucie Höflich, Werner Hinz.

Olympia (1938) (pp. 27–29, 139–142)
Dir: Leni Riefenstahl. *Sc:* Leni Riefenstahl. Documentary in two parts: 1: Fest der Völker; 2: Fest der Schönheit.

Operette (1940) (p. 62)
Dir: Willi Forst. *Sc:* Willi Forst, Axel Eggebrecht. *L.P.:* Willi Forst, Maria Holst, Paul Hörbiger.

Opfer der Vergangenheit (1937) (pp. 89–90)
Dir: Gernot Bock-Stieber. *Sc:* Gernot Bock-Stieber, Dr Frercks.

Paracelsus (1943) (pp. 107)
Dir: G. W. Pabst. *Sc:* Kurt Heuser. *L.P.:* Werner Krauss, Mathias Wieman, Harald Kreutzberg.

Der Postmeister (1940) (p. 43)
Dir: Gustav Ucicky. *Sc:* Gerhard Menzel, from the short story by Alexander Pushkin. *L.P.:* Heinrich George, Hilde Krahl, Siegfried Breuer.

Pour le Mérite (1938) (pp. 52–53, 63)
Dir: Karl Ritter. *Sc:* Fred Hildenbrand, Karl Ritter. *L.P.:* Paul Hartmann, Paul Otto, Fritz Kampers.

Quax, der Bruchpilot (1941) (p. 62)
Dir: Kurt Hoffmann. *Sc:* Robert A. Stemmle, from the story by Hermann Grote. *L.P.:* Heinz Rühmann, Karin Himboldt, Harry Liedtke.

Der Rebell (1932) (pp. 10, 22–23)
Dir: Luis Trenker, Kurt Bernhardt. *Sc:* Robert A. Stemmle, Walter Schmidtkunz, from a script by Luis Trenker. *L.P.:* Luis Trenker, Luise Ullrich, Victor Varconi.

Die Reiter von Deutsch-Ostafrika (1934) (p. 95)
Dir: Herbert Selpin. *Sc:* Marie-Luise Droop, from the novel *Kwa heri. L.P.:* Ilse Stobrawa, Sepp Rist, Peter Voss.

... reitet für Deutschland (1941) (pp. 17–19, 62, 76)
Dir: Arthur Maria Rabenalt. *Sc:* Fritz Reck-Malleczewen, Richard Riedel, Josef

Maria Frank, from the biography of Freiherr von Langen by Clemens Laar. *L.P.:* Willy Birgel, Gerhild Weber, Herbert A. E. Böhme.

Robert Koch, der Bekämpfer des Todes (1939) (pp. 109–111)
Dir: Hans Steinhoff. *Sc:* Walter Wassermann, C. H. Diller, from an idea by Paul Josef Cremers and Gerhard Menzel. *L.P.:* Emil Jannings, Werner Krauss, Viktoria von Ballasko.

Robert und Bertram (1939) (pp. 75, 76)
Dir: Hans Heinz Zerlett. *Sc:* Hans Heinz Zerlett, from the farce by Gustav Raeder. *L.P.:* Rudi Godden, Kurt Seifert, Herbert Hübner.

Romanze in Moll (1943) (p. 15)
Dir: Helmut Käutner. *Sc:* Willy Clever, Helmut Käutner, from a sketch by Willy Clever. *L.P.:* Marianne Hoppe, Paul Dahlke, Ferdinand Marian.

Die Rothschilds (1940) (pp. 75, 76, 78–80, 96–97)
Dir: Erich Waschnek. *Sc:* C. M. Köhn, Gerhard T. Buchholz, from an idea by Mirko Jelusich. *L.P.:* Carl Kuhlmann, Hilde Weissner, Herbert Hübner.

SA-Mann Brand (1933) (p. 34)
Dir: Franz Seitz. *Sc:* Joseph Dalman, Joe Stöckel. *L.P.:* Heinz Klingenberg, Otto Wernicke, Elise Aulinger.

Sieg im Westen (1941) (pp. 57–59)
Dir/Sc: Svend Noldau, Fritz Brunscha.

Spähtrupp Hallgarten (1941) (p. 32)
Dir: Herbert B. Fredersdorf. *Sc:* Kurt E. Walter, Herbert B. Fredersdorf. *L.P.:* René Deltgen, Paul Klinger, Maria Andergast.

Stadt Anatol (1936) (p. 19)
Dir: Viktor Tourjansky. *Sc:* Peter Francke, Walter Supper. *L.P.:* Gustav Fröhlich, Brigitte Horney, Fritz Kampers.

Stukas (1941) (pp. 32–33, 63, 66–67)
Dir: Karl Ritter. *Sc:* Felix Lützkendorf, Karl Ritter. *L.P.:* Carl Raddatz, Albert Hehn, Hannes Stelzer.

Tiefland (1944) (p. 29)
Dir: Leni Riefenstahl. *Sc:* Leni Riefenstahl, from themes suggested by the opera by Eugen d'Albert. *L.P.:* Leni Riefenstahl, Bernhard Minetti, Franz Eichberger.

Triumph des Willens (1935) (pp. 25–27, 29, 134–138)
Dir/Sc: Leni Riefenstahl.

Über alles in der Welt (1941) (pp. 63, 67–68, 75)
Dir: Karl Ritter. *Sc:* Felix Lützkendorf, Karl Ritter. *L.P.:* Carl Raddatz, Hannes Stelzer, Fritz Kampers.

Um das Menschenrecht (1934) (p. 40)
Dir: Hans Zöberlein, Ludwig Schmid-Wildy. *Sc:* Hans Zöberlein. *L.P.:* Hans Schlenck, Kurt Holm, Ernst Martens.

Unter den Brücken (1945) (p. 15)
Dir: Helmut Käutner. *Sc:* Walter Ulbrich, Helmut Käutner, from the script *Unter den Brücken von Paris* by Leo de Laforgue. *L.P.:* Hannelore Schroth, Carl Raddatz, Gustav Knuth.

Unternehmen Michael (1937) (pp. 30–31)
Dir: Karl Ritter. *Sc:* Karl Ritter, Mathias Wieman, Fred Hildenbrand, with Hans Fritz von Zwehl, from the play by Hans Fritz von Zwehl. *L.P.:* Heinrich George, Mathias Wieman, Paul Otto.

Urlaub auf Ehrenwort (1937) (pp. 31–32, 63)
Dir: Karl Ritter. *Sc:* Charles Klein, Felix Lützkendorf, from ideas by Kilian Koll, Walter Bloem and Charles Klein. *L.P.:* Rolf Moebius, Fritz Kampers, René Deltgen.

Venus vor Gericht (1941) (pp. 53, 76)
Dir: Hans Heinz Zerlett. *Sc:* Hans Heinz Zerlett. *L.P.:* Hansi Knotek, Hannes Stelzer, Siegfried Breuer.

Verräter (1936) (p. 96)
Dir: Karl Ritter. *Sc:* Leonhard Fürst, from an idea by Walter Herzlieb and Hans Wagner. *L.P.:* Lida Baarova, Willy Birgel, Rudolf Fernau.

Ein Volksfeind (1937) (p. 51)
Dir: Hans Steinhoff. *Sc:* Erick Ebermayer, Hans Steinhoff, from the play *An Enemy of the People* by Henrik Ibsen. *L.P.:* Heinrich George, Herbert Hübner, Franziska Kinz.

Der Weg zu Isabel (1939) (p. 13)
Dir: Erich Engel. *Sc:* Geza von Cziffra, Frank Thiess, from the novel by Frank Thiess. *L.P.:* Hilde Krahl, Ewald Balser, Maria Koppenhöfer.

Wenn wir alle Engel wären (1936) (p. 16)
Dir: Carl Froelich. *Sc:* Heinrich Spoerl, from his own novel. *L.P.:* Heinz Rühmann, Leny Marenbach, Harald Paulsen.

Wiener Blut (1942) (p. 62)
Dir: Willi Forst. *Sc:* Axel Eggelbrecht, Ernst Marischka, from the operetta by Johann Strauss. *L.P.:* Maria Holst, Willy Fritsch, Fred Liewehr.

Wunschkonzert (1940) (pp. 29, 33, 61, 63, 158–159)
Dir: Eduard von Borsody. *Sc:* Felix Lützkendorf, Eduard von Borsody. *L.P.:* Ilse Werner, Carl Raddatz, Joachim Brennecke.

Yorck (1931) (p. 21)
Dir: Gustav Ucicky. *Sc:* Hans Müller, Robert Liebmann. *L.P.:* Werner Krauss, Rudolf Forster, Grete Mosheim.

Acknowledgments

The film *Wake up, Germany!* was first shown by Norddeutscher Rundfunk on 31 January 1968 in the Third Programme (Norddeutsches Rundfunk) and was repeated on 27 August 1968 on the First Programme. The credits were as follows. Director, Script, Production: Erwin Leiser; Editor: René Martinet; Technical Adviser: Dr Gerd Albrecht. The film was divided into eleven chapters, although these did not correspond with the chapters of the book. The film's commentary has been incorporated into the book.

The author is indebted to the following organisations: Bundesarchiv, Koblenz; Cinémathèque Suisse, Lausanne; Deutsche Kinemathek, Berlin; Deutsches Institut für Filmkunde, Wiesbaden-Biebrich; Document Center, Berlin; Friedrich-Wilhelm-Murnau-Stiftung, Wiesbaden; Gosfilmofond, Moscow; Imperial War Museum, London; Institut für Zeitgeschichte, Munich; National Archives, Washington; Staatliches Filmarchiv der DDR, Berlin; and the National Film Archive, London.

For invaluable assistance and important advice during the preparation of the book and the film the author is grateful to Dr Gerd Albrecht, Hans Barkhausen, Hans Brecht, Rudolf W. Göbel, Dorothea Hollstein, Wolfgang Klaue, Elisabeth Manthey, Hanspeter Manz, Egon Monk, Eberhard Spiess and Herbert Volkmann.

He would also like to record, in grateful memory, the name of Raimond Ruehl, who was the original producer of the film but was killed during the preliminary stages.

Index of Names

9290